THE

BETA
MALE
REVOLUTION

WHY MANY MEN HAVE TOTALLY LOST INTEREST IN MARRIAGE IN TODAY'S SOCIETY

ALAN ROGER CURRIE

Printed on acid-free paper.

Mode One Multimedia, Inc. 2016

http://www.directapproachdating.com
http://www.modeone.net/training/

Other audiobooks, eBooks, and paperbacks by
Author Alan Roger Currie:

Mode One: Let the Women Know What You're REALLY Thinking

Mode One – HARDCORE *(eBook only)*

Mode One – Semantics and Scenarios *(eBook only)*

Oooooh . . . Say it Again: Mastering the Fine Art of Verbal Seduction and Aural Sex

The Possibility of Sex: How Naïve and Lustful Men are Manipulated by Women Regularly *(eBook and audiobook only)*

Upfront and Straightforward: Let the Manipulative Game Players Know What You're REALLY Thinking *(eBook and paperback only)*

THE BETA MALE REVOLUTION

WHY MANY MEN HAVE TOTALLY LOST INTEREST IN MARRIAGE IN TODAY'S SOCIETY

ALAN ROGER CURRIE

Alan Roger Currie

Mode One Multimedia, Inc.
Hollywood, CA 90046

ACKNOWLEDGMENTS

Much love and appreciation to all of my family members, relatives, close friends and loyal supporters of all of my books and talk radio podcast programs. Special acknowledgment always goes to those in my close inner circle of friends, which includes among others, my older brother, Stephen C. Currie

I have a lot of respect for a lot of my fellow authors, bloggers, and experts who have offered knowledge, wisdom, and advice to members of society in the area of dating, interpersonal relationships, marriage, seduction, sex, and other related fields. This list includes among others: Mumia Ali a.k.a. 'Obsidian,' Robert Beck a.k.a. 'Iceberg Slim,' Daniel Bergner, Dr. Brad Blanton, Stephanie Coontz, Dossie Easton, Dr. Warren Farrell, the late Dr. Sigmund Freud, Janet W. Hardy, the late Dr. Alfred Charles Kinsey, the late Dr. William Masters and his late wife, Virginia E. Johnson, Christina Milner, Dr. Richard Milner, Dr. Christopher Ryan, Dr. Helen Smith, Rollo Tomassi *(pseudonym)*, Esther Vilar, and David X.

I have nothing but love for all of the men and women who have been loyal and enthusiastic readers of all of my eBooks and paperbacks, and also nothing but love for all of those who have taken the time out of their busy schedules to listen to multiple episodes of my talk radio podcast program, *Upfront & Straightforward*, my adults-only podcast program, *The Erotic Conversationalist*, as well as one or more of my various audiobooks that are currently available.

I also want to offer a shout-out to all of my male and female clients who feel that my knowledge, wisdom, and general advice has helped them experience a more enjoyable and satisfying love life, sex life, and overall social life. Your Email messages and Facebook inbox messages full of words of kudos and gratitude mean more to me than you'll ever know. Thank you.

Finally, I will always have fond memories of reading books at the Gary (Indiana) Public Library. I loved the Tolleston Branch and Woodson Branch. Reading is Fundamental!

http://www.rif.org/why-books-matter/books-beyond/

TABLE OF CONTENTS

Introduction

This book is going to be a departure from just about all of my previous eBooks, paperbacks, and audiobooks to date. In my previous books, my primary emphasis was on helping single heterosexual men improve their interpersonal communication skills with women, become better at 'verbal seduction' and 'erotic dirty talk' with women, and help men quickly and effectively identify the various forms of 'manipulative head games' that many women tend to employ in today's dating scene.

This book is more of a generalized, unscientific examination of why strictly monogamous marriages used to be appealing for men and women, why the concept of a strictly monogamous marriage has lost a lot of its previous appeal in today's society among both many men and women, and what my strong opinion is on the future of strictly monogamous marriages in the upcoming decades and centuries.

I do not possess a doctoral degree in counseling psychology or relationship therapy, so do not expect any 'deep intellectual analysis' of any sort in this book. I am also not a professional historian or sociologist of any sort by trade, so a lot of my historical facts and assertions may be challenged at some point or be perceived as being 'too general' or 'too broad' and not detailed or substantiated enough. I have no problem with that. **This is a layman's book.** I am going to attempt as much as possible to avoid multiple uses of polysyllabic language and speak to you using very simple easy-to-understand terminology.

In 2009, I was invited to teach an adult education college course at Indiana University Northwest in my hometown of Gary, Indiana entitled *Dating for 21st Century Singles*. The course lasted six weeks, and the length of each class was approximately three hours each. The woman who hired me told me at the time that I was the first person in the entire Indiana University college system to be hired to teach a course related to dating, relationships, sex, and interpersonal communication between the genders that was not an official part of the Gender Studies Department, the Biology Department, the Human Sexuality or Public Health Department, the Psychology Department, and/or the Sociology Department.

If that is indeed a true and valid distinction, then, of course, I feel very honored, and I feel like a 'pioneer' of sorts within the Indiana University college system. I graduated from Indiana University with B.A. in Economics in 1992 with Dean's List Scholar Honors (and I also completed one year of Indiana University's Kelley School of Business Full-Time MBA Program, but I never returned to complete my second year).

In addition to currently being a book author and public speaker, I currently work as a professional men's dating coach (think Actor Will Smith's character in the 2005 romantic comedy, *Hitch*) and I also work as a BDSM and Polyamory lifestyle advisor and consultant for married and unmarried couples who are looking to transition from a traditional monogamous marriage or romantic relationship to one that is openly polyamorous and/or involves a high degree of BDSM influenced 'erotic role play.'

One confession I will offer upfront: When I read many reviews of paperbacks and Kindle eBooks on Amazon.com, some of the reviewers have expressed criticisms such as, *"Save your money! This book is nothing more than a rehash of the author's previous freelance articles, blog posts, internet message board comments and reply-comments, and podcast discussions and talking points. You can find all of those on the internet for free!!"* Critics will probably express similar comments regarding this new paperback of mine.

A lot of the contents of this book is not representative of "new, fresh knowledge and wisdom" from me. A lot of the content of this book comes from the aforementioned *Dating for 21st Century Singles* course I taught at IU Northwest in 2009, past freelance articles of mine from a men's dating advice column I had on the *Examiner.com* between August 2009 and June 2015, past discussion topics from episodes of my talk radio podcast program on the BlogTalkRadio Internet Radio

Network, and a handful of blog articles that I have written and posted on my main website, **DirectApproachDating.com**

Here is the reality of the world we live in today: There are more men and women who are 35 years of age and older who have never been married and do not have any children than at any point in time in the history of the United States. As a guest on my talk radio show expressed in an episode a few years ago, this is the first time in history that there has been a significantly higher number of unmarried women than married women in this country.

Many (heterosexual) women in today's society are not married **by choice**. Either because they have chosen to place more emphasis on their career pursuits or they just feel like marriage is simply not a priority for them. Then there are another group of women who still desire to get married and still hold out the hope of finding "Mr. Right" who will drop to one knee and propose to them, but their biological clock is ticking louder and louder with each year they advance past the age of thirty-five.

Many men I have conversed with in the last fifteen years who are as young as eighteen and as old as their fifties have expressed to me that they have very little if any interest in getting married. Even many of the men who ideally would like to raise one or more children seem to display a very low interest in entering into a strictly monogamous marriage with a woman.

To be quite frank, as of the writing of this book, I would place myself in that category as well. I am 53 years old, and I have never proposed to a woman who was a love interest of mine. Twice, I did at least *entertain* the thought of proposing to a girlfriend of mine – once when I was 21 and a second-time years later when I was 46 – but as time passed in both cases, I decided against it. And I have no regrets about the decision I made in each case. At this time, I also have no children (that I know of). I did impregnate one of my former girlfriends, but she made a 'choice' that she felt was conducive to her objectives at the time.

One of the biggest factors that has lowered my interest in marriage over the years is simply that I do not believe in what I refer to as 'obligatory' monogamy. I only believe in what I refer to as 'natural' and 'organic' monogamy. What is the primary difference between the two types of monogamy?

If you are currently married, engaged, or involved in a long-term 'boyfriend-girlfriend' type romantic relationship, and you have pledged to your spouse, fiancé / fiancée, boyfriend / girlfriend that you have a strong desire to be faithfully monogamous for a long, indefinite period ... but deep-down, you know you have engaged in sex with other partners during your marriage or relationship (i.e., you cheated or committed adultery behind your companion's back) — or at minimum, you have come very, very close to cheating (and still maintain an extremely strong temptation to do so) — then that would represent that you are involved in an 'obligatory monogamous' situation. In other words, 'obligatory' monogamy represents when you do not want to be monogamous to your spouse or romantic companion, but you feel like you 'have to be' or are 'supposed to be' to maintain the interest and companionship of your spouse or a romantic companion.

'Natural' or 'Organic' monogamy would represent a situation where even if your spouse or romantic companion *gave you permission to engage in sexual activities with other people*, **you would voluntarily choose to remain faithfully monogamous to your significant other indefinitely**.

Other than **long-term** strictly **monogamous** cohabitation relationships and marriages between men and women, there are also a) **short-term monogamous relationships** (what some refer to as being a 'serial monogamist'); b) **long-term non-monogamous** (what most refer to as 'Polyamory'); and **short-term non-monogamous** (commonly referred to as being 'promiscuous'). There are some relationships that are not romantic or sexual in nature at all; we simply refer to those as 'purely platonic' relationships or 'friendships'.

The reality is, in the 19th Century and roughly the first sixty years of the 20th Century, the 'strictly monogamous marriage' model was the only one that was universally accepted and approved of publicly in this country. Beginning with 1960 and lasting until 2016, there have now been a number of 'alternative' romantic and sexual relationships that have become very popular among many men and women in society.

This paperback will attempt to enlighten you as to why many men have simply lost interest in the idea of entering into a strictly monogamous marriage or long-term romantic relationship with a woman ... and to a lesser extent, why even more and more women are choosing to remain an 'eternal bachelorette' throughout their entire adult life.

I hope you find the book helpful and enlightening.

Email me with questions and feedback at this Email address: **BetaMaleRevolution@modeone.net**

Continue reading my friend.

Preface:
The Appeal of 'Alpha' vs. 'Beta' males, and How This Affects the Idea of Monogamy and Marriage

For a lot of middle-class and upper-class folk, here is the proverbial 'script' that many men and women look to adhere to:

1) Graduate from high school by no later than the age of 18;

2) Graduate from college by no later than the age of 24;

3) Get engaged and married by no later than the age of 29 (35 years of age at the absolute latest);

4) The man is the designated 'leader' and 'breadwinner' of the household and he finds a job that earns him enough money to provide food, clothing, shelter, and transportation for his wife and children; The woman is the primary 'nurturer' and nanny of the household, and after giving birth to one or more children, she makes sure the house is kept clean and organized, her husband and children receive hot, nutritious meals, and that the children have access to the highest quality of pre-school, grade school, middle school, and high school

education, and she makes sure that the children take care of their designated chores and homework assignments;

5) Once their children graduate from college or graduate school and get married, then their household is considered an 'empty nest' and the married couple grow old together (while enjoying the company of any grandchildren that are born) until they both pass away one day.

This script was, for the most part, adhered to by many men and women beginning with the 18th Century (if not prior) all the way up until roughly the first 60 years of the 20th Century. There are at least a handful of couples who I know that followed chronological points #1, #2, #3, and #4 fully throughout their lives and marriages.

Even for those married couples that chose to bypass college and university life, and chose instead to enter the workforce immediately after high school, many of these couples still generally adhered to this 'life events script.'

LET'S VISIT A HYPOTHETICAL ISLAND FOR A MOMENT

What if each and every woman in society firmly believed in only indulging in strictly monogamous sexual relationships with men? Would that benefit romantic relationships in society? Or would that hurt romantic relationships in society?

What if each and every woman in society believed in was okay and acceptable to engage in promiscuous and polyamorous sexual relationships with men? Would that benefit romantic relationships in society? Or would that hurt romantic relationships in society?

Imagine a scenario where a new social environment was formed with one thousand single women who varied in age between as young as eighteen and no older than thirty-five; also, you had a random selection of one thousand single heterosexual men who varied in age between as young as eighteen and no older than thirty-nine.

Now, imagine each group met up on an island (nicknamed "Monogamy Island"), and after a 'meet and greet' function, each member of both genders were given the rules of the island:

Rule #1: You cannot engage in oral sex, anal sex, and/or vaginal intercourse with any member of the opposite sex for the very first time until you are officially declared as 'coupled up' with a chosen member of the opposite sex; Every action by each man and woman on the island will be monitored by multiple security cameras as well as with GPS-oriented microchip tracking devices implanted underneath the skin of each and every man and woman on the island;

Rule #2: Once you are categorized as 'coupled up' with a chosen member of the opposite sex, you can only engage in sexual activities with that chosen companion, and no one else, for a minimum of one-hundred-and-eighty (180) days; If you violate this rule prior to your 180-day deadline, your status will return to 'single and unattached again,' and you will only be allowed to have sex with a member of the opposite sex who has also violated the 180-day minimum for sexual monogamy;

Rule #3: Every member of the opposite sex on the island will know when they interacted with you exactly how many times you have violated Rule #2 and had your status changed from 'coupled up' to 'single and unattached again';

Rule #4: Any man who impregnates a female companion must remain faithfully monogamous to that same companion until the day he passes away; If a man is caught even attempting to have sex with a woman who is not the mother of his children, he will be placed into the island prison, and never be allowed to engage in sexual relations with anyone for the remainder of his life; Similarly, any woman who is caught even attempting to have sex with a man who is not the biological father of her children will be placed into the island prison, and never be allowed to engage in sexual relations with anyone for the remainder of her life;

Rule #5: Abortions are not allowed; Also, any incidents of rape, date-rape, and sexual assault are punishable by death;

Rule #6: No money is ever allowed to be exchanged on this island; All food, clothing, entertainment, shelter, and transportation are provided for each of the select members of this island;

Rule #7: The longest you can remain on the island without ever have been chosen to be someone's couple partner is twenty years. If no one has chosen you to be their exclusive romantic companion after a twenty-year period, you will be booted off of the island.

Now, you have read all seven rules. If you fell into the appropriate age groups for each gender, would you be motivated to take up residence on this island? Especially if you were guaranteed never to experience any financial struggles or incidents of crime, violence, or poverty?

Let's first examine Rule #1.

If this rule is rigidly enforced, what problems do you see arising from this rule? The first question you would probably end up asking about Rule #1 would be, "Is there a maximum length for the 'coupled up' period if the female partner does not give birth to any children? Nine months? One Year? Two Years? Three Years? Five Years? Longer?" Let's say there is no maximum period if the couple has no children born while they are together.

What if one of the couples who resided on Monogamy Island got along very well when they were not engaged in sexual activities, but sadly, the couple had very little if any sexual chemistry or compatibility? In contrast, what about if another couple that resided on the island has fantastic sexual chemistry and compatibility, but whenever they are not engaged in sexual activities, all they do is argue, argue, argue?

Let's say 'Kevin' and 'Kimberly' are the couple who have exceptional non-sexual chemistry and compatibility, but less-than-average sexual chemistry and compatibility. Then let's say 'Tyrone' and 'Tanya' are the couple who have fantastic sexual chemistry and compatibility, but very disagreeable and highly argumentative non-sexual chemistry and compatibility.

After his sexual monogamy minimum of 180 days with Tanya has expired, Monogamy Island resident Tyrone ends up crossing paths with Kimberly, and later, these two choose to 'couple up.' Tyrone and Kimberly enjoy fantastic and mind-blowing sex, but for Kimberly, her level of non-sexual chemistry and compatibility with Tyrone is not nearly as enjoyable as it was with Kevin. Consequently, every now and then, Kimberly finds herself missing the flattering and entertaining nature of Kevin's accommodating personality and his non-sexual companionship.

Similarly, once Kimberly decided to break things off with Kevin and connect with Tyrone for the next six months, Kevin ends up socially interacting with Tyrone's former lover Tanya, and after a dozen or more 'get to know each other' dates, Kevin and Tanya choose to 'couple up.' Non-sexually, these two get along GREAT. Tanya gets along with Kevin ten times better than she did with Tyrone. These two have no arguments or disagreements with each other whatsoever. Unfortunately, Tanya finds herself reminiscing on the kinky and extremely enjoyable and satisfying sex she experienced with Tyrone quite frequently, despite the non-sexual differences and arguments that she and Tyrone experienced with each other.

Marinate on that scenario for a few minutes.

Next, let's examine Rule #2.

Despite having excellent non-sexual chemistry and compatibility with Kevin, Tanya reaches a point of sexual frustration that she simply cannot tolerate any longer. She ends up aggressively throwing herself at Tyrone and lets him know that she wants to have sex with him behind Kevin's back at least occasionally.

Tyrone knows that given the high level of security monitoring with cameras all over the island, not to mention the GPS tracking devices that have been implanted underneath their skin (these are referred to as 'sexual interaction sensors'), he would never be able to get away with engaging in sex with Tanya behind Kimberly's back without being caught by the Monogamy Island security personnel.

Tyrone has no desire to return to the status of 'single and unattached' and be relegated to being limited to only being able to have sex with other 'Sexual Monogamy Offenders.' Ultimately, Tyrone rebuffs Tanya's sexual advances and chooses to remain monogamous with Kimberly until his 180-day minimum has expired.

Now, Tanya is extremely agitated and sexually frustrated. She still thoroughly enjoys the company of Kevin non-sexually, but sexually, Tanya still yearns for the erotically dominant and uninhibited sexual companionship of Tyrone. Tanya knows if she communicates this to Kevin openly and honestly, there is a great chance that this will ruin her non-sexual chemistry and compatibility with Kevin, so Tanya decides to keep her insatiable lust for Tyrone only known to herself and Tyrone.

Over a period of weeks, Kimberly finds herself constantly whining and complaining about Tyrone's uncompromising dominance outside of the bedroom and also his blatant lack of enthusiasm while engaging in conversation with her and spending time with her when the two are not engaged in sexual activities, but she is willing to tolerate it for the time being because he is providing her with what she feels is the kinkiest and most satisfying sex that she has ever experienced in her life.

As you can surmise, both Kimberly and Tanya have reached a point of frustration in their relationships with Tyrone and Kevin respectively. One woman has a sexual problem in her relationships, and the other woman has a non-sexual problem.

Marinate on this for a few minutes.

Let's take a quick look at Rule #3.

Because of Tyrone's ability to exercise a high degree of sexual self-control and resist the sexual advances of his former companion Tanya, he can continue having sex with Kimberly for the next six months, and then after that, he can couple up with a brand new female sex companion who might be a virgin. This is what keeps Tyrone motivated and self-disciplined.

Kevin is the one who is 'in the dark.' Kevin thought everything was great with Kimberly, but she chose to break things off with him and connect with Tyrone, leaving him confused and heartbroken. Right now, Kevin also believes everything is totally okay with Tanya, but unbeknownst to him, Tanya is greatly missing the sexual companionship of Tyrone.

If Tanya was to be forthright with Kevin about the fact that she misses the sexual companionship of Tyrone, how do you think Kevin would feel after finding this out? His ego would be deeply bruised and for the second time in a row, he would experience a woman breaking his heart. Tanya realizes how hurt Kevin would become, so she chooses to keep her undying lust for Tyrone to herself indefinitely.

Think about Kevin's situation for a minute or two.

Now, let's move on to the trickiest rule of all: Rule #4.

Guess what? Tanya is now unexpectedly pregnant with Kevin's baby. **Kevin is ecstatic.** Kevin had wanted a child with Kimberly, but she always seemed to be reluctant to raise a family with Kevin. Now, Kevin has the family he always wanted with Tanya, which means that – barring an unexpected miscarriage of some sort on behalf of Tanya – Kevin and Tanya have to remain 'coupled up' for **LIFE** according to Monogamy Island rules.

As to be expected, Tanya is full of very 'mixed' emotions. Tanya loves Kevin, but if she is honest with herself, she loves Kevin more like a 'brother' and a 'purely platonic friend' much more than she sees Kevin as a man who she wants to spend **the rest of her life with** both sexually and non-sexually. If nothing else, for strictly sexual purposes, Tanya would very much prefer to be reunited with her former lover Tyrone.

Unlike Kevin, Tyrone has made sure he has taken every precaution to prevent himself from impregnating Kimberly. Tyrone enjoys having sex with Kimberly, but he knows deep-down that he does not want to spend the remainder of his adult life with her. Tyrone wants to engage in as many 180-day short-term monogamous sexual relationships with as many women on the island as he possibly can. The Monogamy Island rules do not prevent Tyrone from becoming a 'serial monogamist.'

If you are a woman reading this paperback right now, can you relate to Tanya's situation? What about Kimberly's situation?

If you are a man reading this paperback right now, whose situation resonates with you more … Tyrone's situation? Or Kevin's (unfortunate) situation?

Think about that for at least a minute or two.

Next, we examine the ultra-sensitive nature of Rule #5.

What if Tanya did not want to give birth to Kevin's son or daughter? What if Tanya does not want to feel 'forced' to remain 'coupled up' with Kevin for the rest of her life? Tanya did not plan to get pregnant … she was simply careless when it came to using birth control methods.

Regardless, on "Monogamy Island," Tanya has no choice but to proceed with the pregnancy and give birth to Kevin's child (with the exception of if she was to experience a very unexpected miscarriage of the child that would be considered "beyond her control"; because of multiple security cameras, she cannot 'force' herself to experience a miscarriage).

If you are a woman reading this paperback, think long and hard on Tanya's predicament. Have you, or a woman you know, ever found herself in a similar situation with a man? I even want my male readers to examine this situation long and hard too. Have you ever impregnated a woman unexpectedly, and you knew deep-down that you had no desire to spend the rest of your life with this woman, and you had no desire even to raise a family with this woman? Marinate on that.

We will now quickly examine Rule #6.

Do you think Tanya would be more motivated to remain with Kevin if he were able to provide her with a much better quality of life than Tyrone would be able to (e.g., a bigger living quarters, more expensive material possessions, higher quality of education for her children, etc.)? This is something to consider.

In this scenario on Monogamy Island, Kevin is unable to offer Tanya any lifestyle and overall quality of life that is any more appealing to her than Tyrone would be able to offer her.

On Monogamy Island, every man and every woman have access to the same overall quality of life, regarding living quarters, quality of food, material possessions and transportation, and quality of education for the children. No one on the island is in possession of more wealth, more material possessions, and more social status than anyone else. Think about that.

For the time being, we will skip examining Rule #7 because it does not validly apply to Tyrone and Kimberly's situation nor does it apply to Kevin and Tanya's situation.

Now, let us return to the real world.

Imagine if the parallel to 'coupling up' on Monogamy Island in the real world society was society heavily promoting the idea of a strictly monogamous marriage between men and women. A strictly monogamous marriage could very well work out for a man and woman who thoroughly enjoy each other's company equally both sexually and non-sexually, and both have a strong desire to raise children together. For couples of this nature, the idea of a strictly monogamous marriage scenario does not present too many challenges or problems at all. This ideal situation between a man and a woman is what most people in society refer to as 'true romantic love.'

On the other hand, when you think of all of the "Kevin" types of the world, the "Tyrone" types of the world, the

"Kimberly" types of the world, and probably most importantly, the "Tanya" types of the world, the idea of a strictly monogamous marriage would appear to potentially create more problems than it solves, wouldn't you say?

Remember when I referred to Kevin as being 'in the dark?' He had no clue that Kimberly broke things off with him because she was not feeling sexually satisfied with him. Similarly, Kevin has no clue that Tanya is also dissatisfied with his companionship sexually and wants to reconnect with Tyrone. Kevin has no clue that Tanya has no real desire to give birth to his child. He is literally "clueless."

Before the days of the internet, many men who were "Kevin" types would remain 'clueless' indefinitely. Then, around 2000, 2001, 2002, the creation of internet message boards and discussion forums geared toward 'men-only issues' gave birth to a world of shared information, knowledge, wisdom and general men's dating advice. We refer to this world of shared information and man-oriented wisdom as "The MANosphere."

Soon, you had the "Tyrone" types sharing their experiences with women with the "Kevin" types. Guys like "Kevin" were like, "Oh my God. Are you KIDDING me?!?" The men who had experiences similar to "Kevin" on Monogamy Island became enlightened, but yet, very angry, hurt, and frustrated.

In the world of the MANosphere, a man of Tyrone's personality and tendencies would be categorized as what is known as an '**Alpha male**.' A man of Kevin's personality and tendencies would is referred to as a '**Beta male**.'

Generally speaking, an *Alpha male* is a man who on the positive end, is very confident, erotically dominant and uninhibited, and exceptionally skilled in the art of pleasing and satisfying women sexually. On the other hand, his controversial qualities are the fact that he is very egotistical to one degree or another, extremely uncompromising, and not at all enthusiastic about spending a significant amount of 'quality time' with women in a non-physical, non-sexual, purely platonic manner. Alpha males are not known for being the exceptionally flattering types, entertaining types, or emotionally empathetic and supportive types. The vast majority of Alpha male types are pretty 'self-absorbed.'

Conversely, the prototypical *Beta male* is a man who, on the positive end, is much easier to get along with personality wise than the average *Alpha male* is, and more often than not, he tends to be much more financially responsible and self-sufficient (and many times, wealthier) than most of the Alpha male types. Also, Beta male types are usually very monogamy-oriented and family-oriented. They usually want to find one good, loyal and monogamous woman, and raise a family with her.

Sadly, one of the primary attributes about Beta male types that is often perceived as 'unappealing' in the eyes of women is that Beta males have no real backbone and they present no real 'challenge' to a woman's ego *(in other words, women generally know that they can 'have their way' with Beta males and influence their behavior and dominate them, and they know they can get away with exhibiting behavior that is spoiled and even somewhat disrespectful to a degree).*

Also, Beta males do not possess nearly as much seductive charm nor as much raw sex appeal as the typical Alpha male does. Their degree of sexual prowess tends to be perceived as 'average' at best, or sometimes even 'less-than-average' in the eyes of most women, with the possible exception of women who are virgins or sexually inexperienced. Beta males are considered to be 'basic,' 'conventional,' and 'vanilla' in bed. Beta males tend to be more loving in bed, more gentle, and even a bit more submissive and accommodating sexually.

If society was set up where it was absolutely mandatory that all men and women could only legally engage in sexual activities with **one sex partner and one sex partner only for their entire adult life**, then the concept of a strictly monogamous marriage would have to be tolerated by the Alpha males (much to their anger and frustration), but it would more-than-likely be to the general liking of the vast majority of Beta male types.

We all know that realistically, this is not the case in the real world. Especially in the 21st Century dating scene.

When it comes to women's desire for highly enjoyable and satisfying sexual companionship, and even more so, if a woman has a strong preference for really 'kinky' and 'raw animal' type sex, just about all women are going to prefer the sexual companionship of an Alpha male over a Beta male.

Studies and surveys conducted with women about their most frequently entertained sexual fantasies have revealed that just about all of the men who (heterosexual) women fantasize about are men who are very Alpha, incredibly masculine, extremely kinky, and unapologetically erotically dominant.

The only women who tend to be content with the sexual companionship of Beta male types are women who are virgins or women who have only engaged in sexual activities with other Beta male types.

On the flip side, when it comes to women's desire for accommodating, flattering and entertaining non-sexual companionship and their desire to have a man provide them with some degree of financial assistance and support as well as a high quality, affluent lifestyle, the vast majority of women are always going to prefer the companionship of Beta male types rather than Alpha male types. Again, Beta male types are also more known for being more family-oriented and monogamy-oriented than the average Alpha male is.

MANY WOMEN WANT TO HAVE THEIR CAKE AND EAT IT TOO

In the world of Erotic Domination & Erotic Submission (i.e., the BDSM lifestyle) and Polyamory, there is an arrangement known as the 'Bull-Cuckold-Hotwife' arrangement.

Men who operate as 'Bulls' for women are men who are very erotically dominant, free-spirited and kinky, usually possess an athletically proportioned and fairly muscular physique, an above-average sized penis, and most importantly, they are very skilled in the art of arousing, pleasing, and satisfying a woman sexually.

Men who function as 'Cuckolds' for women are extremely passive and subservient when interacting with a woman. These men usually earn a high five-figure salary at minimum, and even more so, a six or seven figure salary. Cuckolds are committed to remaining faithfully monogamous to their wife or a romantic companion. They provide their wife or romantic companion with the highest quality of life possible, and if children are involved, they commit themselves to being the best father that a son or daughter could want. Many times, Cuckolds will act as a step-father for the children that a woman conceived with one or more of her Bulls (think about if Kevin, on Monogamy Island, was willing to raise a son or daughter that conceived between Tyrone and Tanya).

The woman who is the 'Hotwife' in this arrangement (even if the woman is unmarried, she is still referred to as a 'Hotwife') experiences the best of both worlds. She has access to one or more Bulls for kinky, enjoyable, and satisfying sex, and she has a wealthy or financially secure 'Cuckold' who will fulfill her every request and satisfy her every non-sexual and financial need.

For all practical purposes, the Bull-Cuckold-Hotwife arrangement is somewhat of a microcosm for how many men and women who are not even involved in the BDSM lifestyle or polyamorous lifestyle are operating these days.

There are many women in today's society who are married to a Beta male type, but these same women are cheating on the Beta male behind-his-back with a man who is more of an Alpha male type. Or, in some cases, a woman may be unmarried but involved in a long-term openly polyamorous relationship with an Alpha male, but this same woman spends the vast majority of her non-sexual free time with one or more of the purely platonic male friends (who are essentially "involuntary Cuckolds") who are in her 'stable' of 'play brothers' and 'male girlfriends.' Some of these platonic male friends even perform a variety of financial and non-financial favors for this woman.

You see, before the days of the internet era, many men in society were not consciously aware of the fact that they were perceived as a 'Beta male' in the eyes of many women. Then, once a lot of knowledge, wisdom, and dating advice began to be offered to men via books, blogs, message boards and discussion forums, and podcast programs, more of the Beta male types began to be awakened and enlightened with what is now referred to as 'Red Pill wisdom' (a reference to the 1999 sci-fi and philosophical thriller, *The Matrix* starring Actors Laurence Fishburne and Keanu Reeves).

In contrast, 'Blue Pill' wisdom would represent a naïve man (or woman) who would buy into the belief that if you placed 1,000 single men on Monogamy Island and 1,000 single women on Monogamy Island, that in a matter of weeks or months, each member of both genders would find their 'soulmate' ... the 'true love of their life' ... couple up ... and live "happily ever after."

Because of the MANosphere, most men who surf the internet regularly and read books written by professional dating coaches (like myself), pickup artists (PUAs), seduction gurus, and masculinity-oriented bloggers, are now consciously aware of the psychological and behavioral differences between the appeal of an 'Alpha male' vs. a 'Beta male' in the eyes of a woman.

Before knowledge and wisdom provided by the MANosphere was available to single heterosexual men, the phrase 'ignorance is bliss' was an extremely valid adage for men who were confirmed Beta male types. Most Beta male types viewed themselves as the 'good guys' in the dating scene. Now, many Beta male types find themselves feeling angry, frustrated, and bitter toward women. They want to avoid being treated like an 'involuntary or unknowing Cuckold' and they have very little interest in being a woman's 'play brother' or 'male girlfriend.' In other words, they do not want to end up like "Kevin" in the fictional Monogamy Island scenario.

The reality of men is, the vast majority of single heterosexual men want to be viewed by women as more of a 'Tyrone' type rather than a 'Kevin' type. At minimum, they want to be perceived as "2/3 Tyrone, and maybe 1/3 Kevin" (this would represent what I refer to later on in this paperback and my other books as an **Alpha male with a few Beta traits and tendencies**).

No heterosexual man who I have ever met in my entire life wants to be known as the 'nice, sweet, easy-to-get-along-with guy' that no women are willing to engage in sexual activities with at least occasionally.

If you are currently married or involved in a long-term romantic relationship with a woman, how can you tell if you are a more of a 'Beta male' type than an 'Alpha male' type?

1)   You practically have to 'beg' your wife, fiancée, or long-term girlfriend for sex on a regular basis. Many times, you're forced to go days, weeks, even months without sexual interaction with your significant other;

2)   Similarly, your wife, fiancée, or long-term girlfriend treats sex almost as if it is a 'reward' of some sort in response to you exhibiting 'good behavior' and performing some financial and non-financial favors for her. Sex is pretty much your 'doggie treat' for the month;

3)   You find yourself frequently feeling 'suspicious' that your wife is cheating on you behind your back because she spends so many evenings and/or weekends away from your place of residence (she usually tells you that she's hangin' out with her girlfriends, but you know better);

Also, your overall sense of the relationship or marriage is that your wife is the one who truly 'wears the pants.'

If you are currently single and unattached, how can you tell if the women you socially interact with perceive you as more of a 'Beta male' type rather than an 'Alpha male' type?

1)   Just about every woman you meet treats you more like a 'play brother' and/or a 'male girlfriend' rather than someone she wants to date or engage in sexual activities with; the women who give you attention always expect you to be accommodating, entertaining, flattering, and polite when you socially interact with them;

2)   Among the women who do seem to be somewhat interested in spending time with you in a more romantic manner, these women are always asking you questions about your level of education or training, your degree of career success, your level of financial success, and ask questions to get an idea of how financially generous you have been with women in your past;

3)   When you express an interest in engaging in any short-term and/or non-monogamous 'casual' sex with women, these women will typically tend to have a very adverse reaction to your sexual advances and refer to your behavior as 'crass,' 'disrespectful,' and/or 'rude';

If any of these symptoms feels familiar, then 99.9% chance, this means that women perceive you as more of a 'Beta male' type than they do an 'Alpha male' type.

A man who is perceived by women as being an Alpha male type rarely if ever has to 'beg' his female companions for sex. If anything, women are known for 'begging' Alpha males for sex. At minimum, women tend to very frequently offer Alpha males the opportunity to have sex with them (monogamous or non-monogamous).

Also, men who are Alpha male types rarely are required to spend a significant amount of money on women to motivate women to agree to have sex with them. Many women will offer to spend their money on Alpha males.

Finally, Alpha male types never allow themselves to tolerate behavior from women that they feel is disrespectful or undesirable in general. If a woman is a 'spoiled' type who is used to having her way with various Beta male types, an Alpha male will very quickly put her in check. Alpha male types have a very strong sense of backbone with women (and other men). Alpha males will leave a woman alone and ignore her indefinitely in a heartbeat rather than allow themselves to tolerate behavior from women that they do not care for.

In my other books, I place all men into **four categories** rather than two. Those four categories are:

· Total Alpha male
· Alpha male with a few Beta traits and tendencies
· Beta male with a few Alpha traits and tendencies
· Total Beta male

Men who are *Total Alpha male* types are the men who women gravitate to for the purpose of strictly sexual companionship (i.e., casual sex). Very few women have a genuine desire to enter into a long-term monogamous relationship or strictly monogamous marriage with men in this category. Mainly because Total Alpha male types are just way too promiscuous and polyamorous for most women's tastes, and these men do not make great non-sexual romantic companions for women.

Men who are an *Alpha male with a few Beta traits and tendencies* types are the category of men who are the most highly desired by women for marriage purposes and long-term 'boyfriend-girlfriend' relationship purposes. These are the men who not only know how to please and satisfy a woman sexually, but they tend to be more relationship-oriented and family-oriented than a *Total Alpha male* type is. On the downside, men in this category are known for being deceitful, duplicitous and adulterous. They will remain with their wife for the long haul, but there is a very good chance that their wives will be cheated on at least a handful of times.

Men who are *Beta male with a few Alpha traits and tendencies* types are the category of men who are the most desired by women for a combination of their accommodating, flattering, and entertaining personalities ... and their desire and willingness to offer women financial assistance and support. Many women feel that they can influence and even 'train' these type of men to be obedient to them and faithfully monogamous to them. Unfortunately, many of the men in this category usually get cheated on by their wives and girlfriends quite frequently.

Men who are *Total Beta male* types are the men in society who are consistently the most romantically and sexually frustrated. Many of these men are referred to as 'losers' and 'incels' (this stands for "involuntarily celibate"), and others in this category tend to be labeled as a 'White Knight' type or a 'Captain Save-a-Ho' type. Men in this category are sometimes completely and indefinitely ignored by women, or if they are given attention by women, they are recruited to be nothing more than a 'play brother' or 'male girlfriend' for women.

Initially, not too many men were consciously aware of the fact that they fell into one of these four categories, but now ... thanks to the knowledge and wisdom shared by myself and other members of the MANosphere in general ... many men are consciously aware of the fact that they are indeed perceived by women as 'Beta male' types.

Many Beta male types in society now want a form of 'revenge' on women. In worst case scenario, the *Total Beta male* types have been involved in incidents of blatant misogyny and violence toward women, such as rape, date-rape, drugging women followed by sexual assault, kidnapping women, and even murdering women.

At minimum, many men who fall into the *Beta male with Alpha traits and tendencies* category are now choosing to ignore women totally, deny women their non-sexual companionship and deny women access to their financial resources and material possessions indefinitely, and limiting themselves to only having sex with women within the context of a short-term and/or non-monogamous sexual relationship. Many of these men have become cynical, discouraged, and jaded toward the notion of 'true love' and the 'living happily ever after' romantic fairy tales that were fed to them as children, teenagers, and young adults by their mothers, aunts, movies, television shows, and media publications. Many Beta male types are **ANGRY**.

Even though a good number of these Beta male types would ideally like to be married and raise a family, many of these now consciously aware Beta males are declaring that they have no desire to propose marriage to a woman who they feel are just looking to exploit them for their financial resources, their accommodating and entertaining personality, and their platonic companionship and emotional empathy and support.

Beta male types now also tend to maintain the assumption that a good number of women in society who are giving them attention are also giving an Alpha male type much easier access to their sexual attention and companionship, whereas these same women are making it extremely difficult for a Beta male type to engage in sexual activities with them without having the Beta male spend a significant amount of money on them and/or offer them a firm promise of indefinite monogamy (i.e., propose marriage to them).

Ladies and Gentlemen, this growing attitude of anger, bitterness, and frustration toward women among Beta male types is what I frequently refer to as **THE BETA MALE REVOLUTION**.

How will THE BETA MALE REVOLUTION affect single women's love life, sex life, and overall social life in the near and distant future?

How will THE BETA MALE REVOLUTION affect dating rituals in the years to come?

Will the BETA MALE REVOLUTION negatively affect the future of strictly monogamous romantic relationships and marriages as well as the family structure in society?

I will attempt to answer all of these questions and more in the remainder of this paperback.

No man wants to be a "Kevin" type any longer. Men want to either be a "Tyrone" type or at minimum, a 'blend' of a Tyrone and a Kevin type.

The **BETA MALE REVOLUTION** has shifted into high gear folks.

Continue reading my friend.

PART ONE:

Understanding Marriage and Its Place in Society

In **Part One**, I will cover the early motivations for why men and women decided to buy into the institution of marriage, and more specifically, why the vast majority of men and women in society only pursued members of the opposite sex to engage in long-term monogamous relationships that would directly lead to a strictly monogamous marriage. I will also touch on how the appeal of marriage began to change in the 1960s and 1970s;

In **Part Two**, I will examine how the impact of the internet and influence of the MANosphere has further delineated the distinction between how women generally respond and react to the romantic and sexual overtures of Alpha males vs. Beta males, and what this means for dating and relationships as well as the appeal of marriage; similarly, I will examine how many men also place women in at least two general categories: a) women who they perceive as prudish and monogamy-oriented 'good girls' and b) kinky and promiscuous 'slut' types.

Then finally, in **Part Three** of this paperback, I will discuss my thoughts on what I feel are many of the 'harsh realities' of today's dating scene, and why I feel that appeal of strictly monogamous marriages has diminished drastically in the last two decades.

Part One is divided into three chapters:

Chapter One
Strictly Monogamous Marriages are NOT for Everyone

Chapter Two
20th Century Factors that Altered the Appeal of Strictly Monogamous Marriages Forever

Chapter Three
Why Organized Religion and the United States Government Will Always Endorse Monogamous Marriages

At the end of this paperback, you will find a list of additional books that I recommend that you read that I offer knowledge, wisdom, and advice that is either directly or indirectly related to the contents I offer in this book.

Continue reading my friend.

Chapter One

Strictly Monogamous Marriages
are NOT for Everyone

Is marriage only for men and who women who have strictly monogamous desires and intentions only? Or is marriage also conducive to the needs and desires of those men and women who have a desire to engage in sexual activities with more than one male and/or female partner?

The average person in American society associates marriage with a strictly monogamous sexual relationship between a heterosexual man and a heterosexual woman. Because both bigamy and polygamy are illegal in the United States, no man even entertains the thought of maintaining a sexual relationship with two or more wives at the same time.

As I alluded to earlier in this paperback, I do not have a problem with what I refer to as 'natural' or 'organic' monogamy, but I have a passionate hatred toward the idea of 'obligatory' monogamy. And that is how I have always viewed the idea of marriage in this country: as a form of obligatory monogamy that is heavily promoted and endorsed by proponents of organized religion, and validated and enforced by the U.S. government.

Some men and women in society believe that Christianity is the only form of organized religion that diligently endorses the idea of strictly monogamous marriages. Well, I would assume that by now that everyone is aware of the fact that there are a good number of men and women who are active members of other forms of organized religion who also favor the idea of strictly monogamous marriages, and there are even a percentage of men and women in this country who are atheists and/or agnostic who have also entered into strictly monogamous marriage unions for years. Strictly monogamous marriages have never been reserved exclusively for Judeo-Christians.

Probably as early as my tenth-grade year in high school, I began to slowly but surely realize that I was not a 'strictly monogamous' type of guy. For example, I remember during the summer months of 1985 when I was a student at Indiana University in Bloomington, Indiana, I many times engaged in sexual activities with as many as five different women in a two-week span. A few of my fraternity brothers and many of the superstar athletes on campus were engaging in sex with even more women than I was on a weekly or monthly basis.

Granted, there are a few men and women I've known over the years who have never had a desire to engage in promiscuous and/or polyamorous sex. Some men and women's natural tendency has always been to limit themselves to strictly monogamous relationships and marriages only. For men and women in that category, I respect them and have no criticisms of their decision to remain faithfully monogamous to one romantic companion or spouse. If a strictly monogamous marriage or long-term romantic co-habitation is what works for them, more power to them.

I would never make the argument that strictly monogamous marriages are a 'bad' thing, but on the other hand, I would never be one to offer a rousing endorsement of strictly monogamous relationships and marriages either. After my parents had passed away, my brother and I were cleaning out my parents' home, and he found an essay I had written for my tenth grade English class when I was in high school.

In that essay, I wrote that I had very ambivalent feelings toward the idea of marriage. For the sake of raising children, I wrote in this essay that I was totally for the idea of finding a wife and getting married someday. On the flip side, regarding the idea of limiting myself to sexual activities with the same woman for the remainder of my adult life, I expressed a total lack of enthusiasm in this 10th-grade essay toward the idea of proposing marriage to a woman at some point in my adult life.

You have to understand: I grew up in an era where Hugh Hefner's *Playboy* magazine was extremely popular. Pornography was just beginning to come into its own. Consequently, the idea of engaging in sexual activities with one woman, and one woman only, for ten years ... twenty years … thirty years or longer was not very appealing to me at all. Even as far back as the 10th grade, I regularly envisioned myself leading a very promiscuous and/or polyamorous sex life with women for most of my twenties and thirties, and even most of my forties. I actually viewed one of my fraternity brothers, NBA professional basketball legend **Wilt Chamberlain** as an idol of mine when it came to his approach to women (Chamberlain reportedly engaged in sexual activities with as many as 20,000 women over the course of his life, and he never once got married before he passed away in 1999; I actually met Chamberlain once in 1995 in Los Angeles). Chamberlain is quoted in interviews in saying that he was never going to 'pretend' to be interested in long-term monogamy when he knew within himself that long-term monogamy was simply not his thing. I feel the same way.

Only the part of me that has maintained a strong desire to be a parent to at least one son or daughter, and have someone in my life to help me raise that child, has led to me frequently entertaining the thought of marrying someday (as of the publishing of this paperback, I have yet to be married, and I also have yet to be a parent).

In early January of this year, I began researching some of the general origins of marriage and the history of marriage in this country in preparation for an 'Open Forum Discussion' episode of my talk radio podcast program entitled, "If Marriage is So Great, Why So Many Divorces? If Marriage is So Bad,

Why So Many Weddings?" I received a lot of feedback from my male and female listeners in response to this particular episode.

Some of what I learned about the history of marriage during my brief, informal research totally surprised me. For example, many people in today's society are under the misguided assumption that polyamory is more or less a 'new' form of alternative sexual relationships between men and women. Not hardly. Many men and women in the history of the world engaged in promiscuous sexual behavior and polyamorous sexual behavior before society ever fully endorsed and accepted the idea of men and women joining via marriage.

Marriage became popular among the masses primarily because of two major reasons:

1) Men who were previously promiscuous and/or polyamorous began to become 'insecure' regarding the issue of paternity; marriage was a way to cause men to feel more reassured that the children who they thought were theirs were (DNA paternity testing did not come into play in society until the 1960s);

2) Marriage became very conducive to many men who wanted to transfer ownership of their wealth, their personal property, and other assets and material possessions to someone once they passed away.

What I also found out while conducting informal research on marriage in centuries prior was that there were many married men in past centuries whose wives actually approved of them maintaining one or more mistresses as long as those mistresses did not allow themselves to get pregnant, and those mistresses promised the wives not to attempt to 'steal' their husbands away from their wives and be respectful and deferential to the wives.

A *courtesan* would be an example of one type of mistress or additional lover that many wives would approve of their husbands maintaining a discreet relationship with. The modern day equivalent of a courtesan would be a professional Call Girl or upscale Erotic Escort who has a married man as a regular client, and that man's wife knows about the relationship and has given the husband permission and approval to carry on with the Call Girl or Erotic Escort indefinitely as long as the relationship between them remains very private and discreet.

Similar to a courtesan, another type of mistress that many wives approved of was what is known as a *concubine*. A concubine is a married man's additional lover (or 'openly known mistress') who frequently spends the night at the residence of the married couple, and in many cases, lives with the married couple indefinitely. As we all know, in today's society, prostitution is illegal in most states (Nevada is a known exception), but the concept of concubinage is still legal.

In many cultures and countries, polygamous marriages were far more popular and more widely accepted than strictly monogamous marriages. To this day, there are many cultures who frown on the idea of strictly monogamous marriages. Why? Because of **pure numbers**.

For example, if you placed 1,500 single heterosexual men on an island with 2,500 single women, and everyone's objective was to enter into a long-term strictly monogamous relationship or marriage, then that would mean that 1,000 women would essentially be left out in the cold. And this is exactly why many people who live in cultures where there are far more single women than single men (or vice versa) are totally against the idea of strictly monogamous marriages.

If polygamy was legal in the United States, more than likely, men who are considered to be uneducated, erratically employed, full of financial problems and bad credit, and were perceived to be boring and/or unsatisfying in bed would never, ever find a wife. Even with anti-polygamy laws in place today, there are many men who still struggle to connect with women romantically or sexually. This is one of the primary reasons why I felt motivated to publish this paperback.

If you are a woman reading this paperback right now, let me ask you a question: If you were on an island, and it was just you and three equally attractive men ... would you commit yourself to remaining strictly monogamous with just ONE of those three men? Or would you share yourself sexually with all three men?

What if you did only choose one of the three men to engage in sexual activities with, and the other two men conspired to murder the one man you chose to be your exclusive sexual companion? Would you end up regretting that decision?

If you are a man reading this right now, let me ask you a similar question: If you were on an island, and it was just you and three equally attractive women ... would you choose only to engage in sexual activities with just ONE of those three women? Or would you offer your sexual companionship to all three women equally? (for many men reading this paperback, this will appear to be a very dumb question on my part)

What if one of the three women said, "I will only have sex with you if you remain strictly monogamous to me," but the other two women let you know that having sex with both of them was not a problem for them. What would you do? Ignore the one woman who desires strict monogamy in favor of the two women who are open to polyamorous sex? Would you opt to remain strictly monogamous with the one woman who demanded it? (I know ... another dumb question) Or would you choose to have sex with the woman who demanded strict monogamy, but find a way to cheat on her with the other two women behind her back?

The reason I ask these questions is because I have had a good number of men and women confess to me that over half of the reason why they have maintained the disingenuous façade of being interested in a strictly monogamous marriage was because of the influence, opinions, and expectations of **other people** and society as a whole rather than a decision that they arrived at because of **their** true desires and interests.

For example, I know many women who got married because their mother, step-mother, father, or step-father basically 'pressured' them to get married by a certain age. They were not enthusiastic about the idea of getting married. Many of them married spouses who they were not really in love with. They just got married to please their parents. Some men have told me the same thing.

My late father never put pressure on my brother or me to get married. Never. My late mother did, at least to a small degree. She wanted grandchildren very, very badly. Especially once she passed the age of 60. A part of me regrets to this day not being able to provide her with the joy of interacting with and spoiling a grandson or granddaughter. I mean, I could have just chosen some random girlfriend and got her pregnant, but my mother was vehemently against the idea of me or my brother impregnating women outside the context of marriage, even though she had many nephews and nieces who produced children out of wedlock.

It was not so much that my mother was exceptionally self-righteous or judgmental, but the vast majority of parents from her generation and her parents' generation felt the same way. In today's society, it is not too big of a deal for a woman to give birth to a son or daughter outside the context of marriage.

But in the early-to-middle part of the 20th Century and prior, it was considered extremely embarrassing and shameful to a man and woman to have their daughter get pregnant or have their son impregnate a woman without being married first.

This is where the term 'shotgun wedding' originated. Many fathers would become incredibly angry if a young man had sex with their daughter without being married to her. If their daughter came up pregnant, the woman's father would come to the house of the young man who impregnated his daughter and threatened the father of the boy and the boy himself. The father would say, *"You better propose marriage to my daughter and make an honest woman out of her, and do so immediately … or else, I am willing to go to prison after I blow your head off with this shotgun!!"*

Speaking of women's overprotective fathers, what most people in today's society do not realize is that marriage was not initially associated with the notion of 'true love' and 'romance' like it is today. Marriage has become very much 'commercialized' in today's society. If you conduct your research on the origins of marriage, you will quickly realize that 'true love' was not the primary basis for marriage when marriage was still in its early stages.

There was a time in previous centuries where marriage was viewed as more of a 'business transaction' between the father of the bride and the father of the groom than it was a 'love connection' between the bride and groom.

You see, before the days of feminism leaving its strong stamp on society, women were considered a man's 'property.' Women essentially had no personal rights in society (which is ultimately what led to the First and Second Wave of Feminism).

A man's daughter was very much considered his "property." A woman did not own her body. Her father did. A woman's father decided when his daughter could kiss a boy, if and when his daughter could accept an invitation from a boy to go out on a date, and if that boy / young man could eventually propose marriage to her. Before 1960, the vast majority of women could not choose their husbands and romantic companions in the manner that you see women doing that today. **Not at all.**

Originally, marriage was almost more beneficial to the parents of the bride and groom in many ways than it was for the married couple themselves. Even in today's society, in certain cultures, they still have what is known as 'pre-arranged marriages.' This is a situation where the parents of the bride have a discussion with the parents of the groom, and it is the parents who arrive at the decision that their son and daughter should marry each other. The bride and groom end up having very little say-so in the matter.

A woman who was not a virgin at the time of her wedding was very frequently perceived as "damaged goods" and in some cases, 'unmarriageable.' Many parents would refuse to allow their son to marry a woman who had already engaged in sexual activity before her wedding day.

That is no longer the case in today's society. Now, technically, a woman is on her own once she turns 18 years of age. No woman's father is legally responsible for the financial well-being of his daughter once she turns 18 years of age (even though realistically, many fathers in today's society do still take care of their daughters financially far past the age of 18).

What a wedding represented was a "transfer of property" (a man's daughter) from the father of the bride to the bride's soon-to-be-husband. The parents of the bride and groom honestly could care less if the bride and groom were actually 'in love' with one another. That was a very secondary concern to the parents of the groom or the parents of the bride.

For those men and women who wanted to get married for purposes of 'true love' without their parents' consent, they resorted to something known as *eloping*. To elope meant that you were defying the wishes of your parents, and you went ahead and got married without your mother or father's blessing. Parents would become livid with anger if they found out their son or daughter had eloped. Many parents would totally cut off their children financially if they chose to elope.

In today's society, very few men and women continue to elope. The vast majority of women in today's society will marry any man they choose to. They could care less about what their mother or father thinks unless their parents are extremely wealthy and providing them with a high degree of financial support well into their adult years.

As I told my students in my *Dating for 21st Century Singles* course in 2009, the two decades that caused the appeal of strictly monogamous marriages to begin slowly declining was that period between 1960 and 1979. When you combine new and improved birth control methods (particularly, the birth control pill), Second Wave Feminism, the 'Sexual Revolution' (or what some refer to as the 'Sexual Liberation Movement'), and the legalization of abortion, many men and women's long-held beliefs and attitudes toward the idea of entering into a strictly monogamous marriage changed **forever**.

I will go into detail in the very next chapter about how a lot of what transpired between 1960 and 1979 profoundly affected men and women's general attitudes toward marriage and monogamy forever.

Continue reading my friend.

Chapter Two

20th Century Factors that Altered the Appeal of Strictly Monogamous Marriages Forever

World War I (1914-18) and World War II (1939-45) had a major impact on many married couples. A lot of married women with children were left widowed because their husbands died during active duty protecting our country. This was arguably the highest number of widowed wives with children since the American Civil War (1861-65).

One thing I mentioned on my talk radio program was that the first time the notion of modern day polyamorous sex first came to public attention nationally was during World War II.

Some soldiers were interviewed anonymously by a major media publication, and confessed that because they were gone for months away from their wives, they would invite a close male friend of theirs (often another soldier who was not currently involved in a tour of active duty) to have sex with their wife until they returned home.

These United States Armed Forces soldiers were realistic enough to recognize that their wives would become extremely horny if they went too long without sexual activity, so their attitude was, "I would rather my wife engage in sexual activities with a man I know and trust than to engage in sexual activities with some complete stranger."

Then later, the friend (who in most instances, was married or engaged himself) would usually 'return the favor' once he became actively involved in a tour of duty. This arrangement between these trusting soldiers is what essentially set the stage for what later came to be referred to as 'swinging' and 'couple-swapping,' which are two very popular forms of openly polyamorous sexual relationships between men and women, and particularly married couples.

It was approximately fifteen years after the end of World War II when the dating and relationships landscape began to change. The two decades which had arguably the most profound effect on the concept of marriage, monogamy, sex and general dating rituals between heterosexual men and women was that period between **1960-69** and **1970-79**. Just about every aspect of modern dating rituals that is present in today's society began forming in the 1960s and 1970s.

THE BIRTH CONTROL PILL

Remember when I talked about parents frowning on their sons and daughters engaging in sex before marriage? Realistically, there was always a small percentage of men and women who simply could not wait until marriage to have sex for the first time. Their raging hormones would get the best of them.

As I have mentioned time and time again in my other books, the desire for sex is a very strong hormonal desire. You cannot intellectualize sex or attempt to legislate sexual desire. Sexual desire is what it is, similar to the desire for food and beverages.

Unlike modern day dating, very few women before roughly 1960 wanted to admit publicly that they were pregnant without being married first. If a woman did get pregnant outside the context of marriage, they would many times seek to have an abortion, which at the time, was very much illegal.

By 1960, condoms were already in play, as were diaphragm sponges, among other practiced methods of birth control methods. The most profound birth control method introduced into society in this decade was the **Combined Oral Contraceptive Pill (COCP), otherwise known as simply 'the birth control pill.'**

Even though the birth control pill was not considered to be a "100% guaranteed" method of preventing pregnancy, it was considered to be just as effective, if not more effective, than using condoms and other modern birth control methods.

The birth control pill opened the door for many men and women to feel more comfortable engaging in premarital sex, even though the nation's religious factions, as well as many middle-class and upper-class parents still frowned on such behavior (especially regarding their daughters).

Even though many parents did not want their daughters engaging in sex before marriage, they were objective-minded enough to realize that having their daughters take the pill was a much better option than having their daughter get pregnant and then lean toward the high risk and complications of having an illegal abortion.

SECOND WAVE FEMINISM

The First Wave of Feminism which began in the 19th Century was primarily about women wanting to be viewed as 'fully dimensional human beings' rather than simply 'men's property.'

The Second Wave of Feminism had more to do with women wanting to have the same access to employment opportunities and wage-earning opportunities as men. Also, among other contributing factors, women wanted to dictate their own romantic and sexual choices rather than have their fathers, step-fathers, or husbands dictate those choices.

You have to understand that because women could not gain employment in the same way that a man could, and they could not in most cases earn the same wages as a man, they were forced to rely on men for their financial security.

Well, what if a woman did not want to get married? What if a woman wanted to give birth to children without being married? What if a woman was bisexual or a lesbian? What if a woman wanted to take on an additional lover to her husband, just as many men had additional lovers and mistresses for centuries?

These questions and the answers to these questions is what fueled the Second Wave of Feminism. Truth? I cannot blame women for wanting their individual rights and equal employment opportunities and wage-earning opportunities. I have no problem with those feminist objectives at all.

Unlike me, many men in society did have problems with the Feminist Movement. Many men knew that if women could get a job just as easily as they could, and could earn just as much if not more money than them, then what would be women's motivation to behave in an obedient and submissive manner toward their husbands and future husbands? What would be a woman's motivation to function as a 'stay-at-home mother' and 'housewife?'

Bottom line, women wanted to be in a position in which they could have sex whenever they wanted to and with whomever they wanted to, without their fathers, step-fathers, and men in general having a say so in the matter.

There are many men who strongly believe that society is likely to experience a high degree of problems when a high number and high percentage of the women become promiscuous and sexually out-of-control. Generally speaking, men have always wanted to maintain a certain degree of 'control' and 'influence' over women's sexual behavior. Again, this is how things were before the First and Second Wave of Feminism took place. Men pretty much influenced almost every aspect of women's behavior in this country before feminism took over.

THE SEXUAL REVOLUTION

Technically, what is known as the 'sexual revolution' and/or the 'sexual liberation movement' began before the 1960s, but it was in the 1960s – when combined with the Second Wave of Feminism and the introduction of the birth control pill – when it shifted into high gear.

There was always a faction of society that believed in what was known as 'The Free Love Movement,' which was all about anti-monogamy and anti-marriage. Men and women who loved the 'Free Love' mindset felt right at home during the Sexual

Revolution. Critics of the Sexual Revolution and Free Love Movement felt that promiscuity and polyamory would totally destroy the moral fabric of society, lead to a higher number of abortions, result in more sexually transmitted diseases, and ultimately destroy the family structure because women would end up giving birth to too many children fathered by a number of different men outside the context of marriage.

More and more women began to feel more comfortable engaging in sexual activities before marriage, outside the context of marriage, and with multiple male partners (and female partners too) during the Sexual Revolution.

THE LEGALIZATION OF ABORTION

First men and women would use the 'withdrawal' method in an attempt to avoid premarital pregnancies; then they turned to condoms, diaphragm sponges, and a handful of other methods; then came the birth control pill.

What if none of these methods worked? What if a man persuaded a woman to allow him to have sex with her 'raw dog' style (i.e., engage in unprotected sex) and he inadvertently got the woman pregnant when neither one of them wanted to raise a child together nor were in a financial position to raise a child together?

Abortions have been around for centuries, but once again, in most countries and cultures, they were illegal and usually performed 'secretly' to avoid legal consequences.

In 1973, all of that changed when the Supreme Court voted 7-2 for legalizing abortion. Two legal cases – *Roe v. Wade* and *Doe v. Bolton* – contributed to this decision. Now, abortions were legal in all fifty states of this country.

Women who were feminists were highly in favor of this decision. Feminists feel as though women should be able to make any decision they desire when it comes to their body. Critics categorized abortion as 'legalizing the murder of an unborn child.' To this day, most members of the religious community are harshly critical of abortion, except when a woman is a victim of rape and incestuous molestation.

PORNOGRAPHY

Even though pornographic films existed before 1970, they did not become popular until the 1970s. *Deep Throat*, released in 1972, was one of the first pornographic films ever to have a large audience come to an adults-only movie theater to view it. Other titles that were popular were *Behind the Green Door* and *The Devil in Miss Jones*.

Andy Warhol, the famed American artist, has been credited with releasing the first major feature-film in movie theaters that included very explicit sex scenes. Warhol's film was entitled *Blue Movie,* and it was released in 1969. Another similar film was *Last Tango in Paris* which was released in 1972.

In the very next chapter, I will discuss how a minimum of two major entities in society tend to benefit from the idea of promoting marriage, and particularly, strictly monogamous marriages: Organized Religion and the U.S. Government.

Continue reading my friend.

Chapter Three

Why Organized Religion and the United States Government Will Always Endorse Monogamous Marriages

If the United States Supreme Court decided to pass a law that totally abolished the institution of marriage, what groups of people in society would this decision be most detrimental?

Would grocery stores, fast-food restaurants, and fine dining restaurants lose business if men and women were prevented from getting married? No.

Would clothing stores, shoe stores, and furniture stores lose business if men and women were prevented from getting married? No.

Would automobile dealerships or the travel industry lose money if men and women were prevented from getting married? No.

Jewelry stores that sell engagement rings and wedding rings would take a hit. I doubt if they would be forced to go out of business, but their revenues would drop a bit.

Tuxedo shops and wedding gown shops would take a hit. Even unmarried men rent tuxedos from time to time, but wedding gown stores would be forced out of business.

Limousine businesses would take at least a small hit. Surely not so much that they would be put out of business though.

Some retail stores where friends of the married couple purchase wedding gifts might suffer some decrease in revenues, but not so much that they would find themselves out of business.

Okay. All of those vendors above aside, just who in society would be the most negatively affected if marriage became illegal in the United States?

At bare minimum, there are two major entities in society that would suffer if marriage was completely abolished: **organized religion** and the part of **local, state, and federal government** that handles estate taxes and transference of personal property and material assets after a man or woman's death.

ORGANIZED RELIGION

From the time I was in pre-school all the way up until roughly 1996, I was an enthusiastic supporter of organized religion and Christianity. Then, after an experience being involved with a 'cult-like' church in Los Angeles between July 1994 and December 1996, the idea of being involved with organized religion left a very bad taste in my mouth.

Now, I consider myself more 'spiritual' than 'religious.' I still believe that spirituality, and even organized religion, does its job in those instances when they help men and women reduce their violent tendencies, when they discourage men and women from giving in to the temptation to engage in criminal and illegal activities, and just generally when they encourage men and women to treat their fellow human beings with a higher degree of respect, objectivity, love, and empathy.

There are many religious sermons expressed by ministers, reverends, pastors, and other church leaders that primarily focus on the idea of getting married, and remaining faithfully monogamous to your spouse until the day you pass away.

Many men and women enthusiastically give away ten percent or more of their income to churches all across the nation because being a regular church member makes them feel like they are 'good people with good hearts and good intentions.'

I cannot tell you how many sexual hypocrites I have met in my life who were active members of churches. Some of the kinkiest, most highly promiscuous women I have ever interacted with were women who attended church each and every Sunday.

I met a woman a few years ago who was recently divorced from her husband who was a minister at a church in a Midwestern state. Why did she divorce her very religious husband? Because this man had engaged in sexual activities with as many as forty women in his church. FORTY WOMEN. Here is a man who is supposed to be preaching AGAINST the idea of lust, fornication, and premarital sex, and this man was having sex with over three dozen women. A good number of the women her husband had sex with were married (it was some of the married women that first came forth and confessed to this woman that they were sleeping with her husband).

In my hometown of Gary, Indiana, there have been numerous stories – many confirmed, and some rumored – of ministers and church leaders committing adultery on a regular basis. Some ministers were written up in the local newspapers for impregnating young women while they were married.

I know many men who are married that would never want their wives talking to a male church leader about the problems in their marriage or the frustrations of their sex life. Never. Ever. This is how many of these scandalous, adulterous church leaders end up having sex with married women and engaged women. They get these naïve, unsuspecting women to open up and discuss their feelings of loneliness, betrayals by men, and guilty feelings of lust and confessions of female masturbation while watching pornography. Next thing you know, that woman develops an 'emotional bond' with her church leader, and she lowers her guard, and the church leader then seduces her.

I am sure there are many male church leaders who exhibit nothing but the highest degree of moral character and integrity, but there is definitely a percentage of church leaders that are nothing more than 'snakes in the grass' and 'wolves in sheep's clothing.' Believe that.

Organized religion would totally lose credibility - and along with that, revenue - if they were to ever openly and enthusiastically endorse the idea of cohabitating without being married, premarital sex, promiscuous sex, openly polyamorous marriages and relationships, or same-sex marriages.

Realistically, organized religion would probably lose hundreds of millions of dollars, if not billions of dollars, nationwide if various ministers across the country began saying that it is 'okay' and 'acceptable' to engage in any sexual relationship other than a strictly monogamous marriage between a heterosexual man and a heterosexual woman.

Organized religion is the basis for most of society's sense of morals, ethics, values, and personal principles. Also, the vast majority of weddings still take place in churches and other venues of worship, and those places make money off of those weddings by renting out their facilities.

Many ministers, pastors, and other religious leaders are to promoting marriage and monogamous sexual behavior what many pickup artists (PUAs) and professional seduction gurus are to promoting promiscuous and/or polyamorous sexual behavior. That is how they earn a large part of their living.

If it were announced tomorrow that the United States Government was on the verge of permanently abolishing the institution of marriage, the first group of protestors would more-than-likely be those heavily involved with organized religion.

Why would you need to listen to a sermon about "containing your lust" if you were free to indulge in non-monogamous sexual behavior? Why would you need to listen to a sermon about the sins of adultery if there was no such thing as marriage? Why would you need to listen to a sermon about avoiding premarital sex and sex with someone other than your husband or wife if marriage was abolished and illegal?

The 'powers that be' in organized religion **know** that most men and women are going to give in to their lustful desires and their adulterous temptations. **They know this**. And they bank on being there to 'consult' these men and women who are experiencing problems in their marriage and problems remaining faithfully monogamous to their spouse just like a lawyer banks on consulting men and women with legal problems and physicians bank on consulting those with health problems.

Also, churches are probably the top venue where many single men visit to find a 'good woman' (i.e., a woman with good moral character who places a high emphasis on loyalty to men and strict monogamy), and similarly, many single women feel as though the church is where they experience the best chance of meeting a 'good man' (same attributes as a 'good woman' with an added emphasis on the man being financially self-sufficient).

When most men and women think about an American institution that highly encourages them to become and remain good husbands, good wives, and good parents, the number one place they think about is one or more of their local churches or a similar place of worship and organized religion.

Organized religion would never, ever want to see marriage abolished. Not in a trillion years. The idea of marriage, and more specifically the idea of a strictly monogamous marriage, is one of the primary cornerstones of organized religion.

Only one other major entity in society would never want to see the Unites States Government abolish marriage . . . and that is **the United States Government itself**.

THE UNITED STATES GOVERNMENT

Unlike organized religion, the U.S. Government does not want to keep marriage legal to make money or to earn some sort of profit. The U.S. Government is going to always receive their fair share of tax revenues. With them, it is more so about *keeping issues of personal property and material assets organized and reducing incidents of male violence due to sexual jealousy and envy as well as non-existent or irresponsible parenting.*

Truthfully, the U.S. Government could care less about how many men or women you choose to have sex with. In their minds, that is **your** business. They don't care if you love Brenda or Michelle, and they don't care if you're having sex with Daniel or David. The U.S. Government could give a rat's ass.

If you own a nice house with $200,000 worth of assets and a nice 401k retirement plan in place, the U.S. Government wants to know who do you want to transfer ownership of your house to when you pass away? Who gets to claim ownership of your automobiles, furniture, and other material possessions once you die? What person becomes eligible to receive your social security benefits and/or retirement plan benefits after you have passed away? Who will be responsible for paying the property taxes on your house until it is sold? These are the primary issues that the United States Government cares about.

Let's say you are a womanizing bachelor who has five different women who each gave birth to a child that you impregnated them with. Then, unexpectedly, you die. If you passed away with a nice big house and a number of expensive cars, each of those women who are the mothers to one of your children is going to want to claim ownership to those items. Especially if you have no parents and/or siblings alive at the time of your death.

One woman will say, "Well, he cared about ME the most!! So, I deserve to claim ownership to his house!!" Another woman will say, "He and I had sex 2-3 times per week every week ... so I feel that I deserve to claim ownership to that big beautiful house of his!!" Now, at minimum, if you have at least one son or one daughter who is 18 years of age or older at the time of your death, the U.S. Government knows who falls in line to inherit your material possessions and personal property.

In a situation where you had no parents or siblings alive at the time of your death and no (adult) children, but you had a number of different sexual lovers who are all claiming that you loved them the most, and therefore they deserve a large portion of your material assets, this does nothing but cause the U.S. Government an unnecessary headache in terms of legalities, paperwork, and taking the time to resolve disputes.

You passing away with a wife or husband left behind who is still alive makes things a heck of a lot easier for your city government, county government, state government, and the federal government to pass on your property and possessions without having to resolve any major disputes or arguments. Especially if you did not have a last will and testament in place.

Also, an emphasis on strictly monogamous marriages ultimately leads to less violence in society. Remember that island scenario I presented to you where I said if one attractive, sexy woman was on an island with three men, but she was only willing to have sex with one of the three men? 99.9% chance, the other two men would murder that one man who had gained the opportunity to enjoy himself sexually with the one woman on the island. That is just the nature of men. For most men, there is a direct correlation between how romantically and sexually frustrated a man is, and how competitive and/or violent he is.

Also, when children have abusive, argumentative, or irresponsible parents, this is another factor that will ultimately lead to those children growing up to become violent and prone to engage in criminal activities. Studies show that most men and women who were brought up in single-parent homes are more likely to engage in criminal activity and violent activities as teenagers and adults than those who were raised in a two-parent home. **The U.S. Government is well aware of this.**

So, bottom line, organized religion wants you to get married and remain married because it gives their sermons more credibility, and in most cases, leads to them attracting more members and receiving higher monetary contributions from married couples, engaged couples, and/or those single men and women who are seeking to find someone to marry. The men and women who attend churches on a weekly basis know that they possess a high degree of lustful and adulterous desires and temptations, so they look to the church leaders to provide them with much-needed encouragement, guidance, and self-discipline.

The U.S. Government would prefer that you get married and remain married so that it can keep your financial and material resources more organized once you pass away, and make it easier for your personal property, material possessions, and retirement benefits to be transferred to your living spouse and heirs after your death. Also, the U.S. Government wants to help reduce the number of incidents of men acting out in a criminal and violent manner due to a high degree of romantic and sexual frustration on their part or bad parenting.

In the chapters in Part Two of this book, I will examine how many of the activities both before 1960 and surely after 1960 have led to men placing women into a minimum of at least two distinct categories, and women – consciously or subconsciously – have pretty much done the same thing with men.

Women, generally speaking, tend to be viewed as either a prudish and monogamy-oriented 'good girl' ... or a kinky and promiscuous or polyamorous 'slut.'

Similarly, as mentioned already, men are typically treated by women as either an 'Alpha male' or a 'Beta male.'

Continue reading my friend.

PART TWO:

'Good Girls' vs. 'Kinky Sluts' and 'Alpha Males' vs. 'Beta Males'

In **Part Two**, I will examine how men tend to place women into at least two categories, and how women tend to do the same thing with men. Among those who cheat and commit adultery, these categories play a **SIGNIFICANT** role in motivating men and women to lie, to be disingenuous and sexually duplicitous, and engage in manipulative 'head games' with one another.

<u>Part Two is divided into four chapters:</u>

Chapter Four
A Brief Look Back at 'Monogamy Island'

Chapter Five
Examining the Appeal of Prudish, Monogamy-Oriented 'Good Girls' vs. Kinky, Promiscuous 'Sluts'

Chapter Six
The Role Alpha Males and Beta Males Fulfill for Women

Chapter Seven
The Emergence of The Beta Male Revolution

Continue reading my friend.

Chapter Four

A Brief Look Back at 'Monogamy Island'

Right now, take a few minutes to refresh your memory on the concept of my fictional scenario entitled 'Monogamy Island' in the Preface Chapter. Return here – Chapter Four – once you have re-read the general social constructs I presented in the Preface (in case you are very young and reading this book, and you are not familiar with the term 'social construct,' this represents a way of living and interacting with other human beings that may seem 'normal' and 'natural,' but in reality, this way of living and interacting with others was created and brainwashed into your mind by people with power and influence).

If you notice, on Monogamy Island, once a man impregnated a woman, that couple will have to remain sexually monogamous to each other from the time the woman got pregnant up until the time one of the two passed away.

Even without children, each couple had to remain sexually monogamous for a minimum of one-hundred-and-eighty days, or else they would be relegated to only being able to have sex with members of the opposite sex who also did not have the sexual self-control and self-discipline to remain monogamous to their designated romantic companion for at least 180 days.

In other words, just about every man and woman who resided on Monogamy Island would eventually fall into two categories: the men and women have the desire and discipline to remain very monogamy-oriented, and those men and women whose promiscuous and/or polyamorous tendencies got the best of them and caused them to 'fail' at the objective of remaining monogamous.

A scenario such as this would ultimately create two 'classes' of men and women. In the real world, the combination of a man or woman's family background, their level of accumulated wealth and career success, their level of intelligence, knowledge, wisdom, and formal academic education achieved, and their lack of involvement in acts of violence and/or criminal activities tends to heavily contribute to their 'socio-economic class.'

A person who is intelligent, usually highly educated, extremely wealthy (or at minimum, their parents are very wealthy), and who has never been convicted of a major felony (and particularly, a violent felony) is generally considered to be included in what is known as 'high society,' or what many sociologists refer to as 'the upper class' of the United States.

A person who is intelligent, usually formally educated (i.e., attended and graduated from college or achieved some vocational training), and is gainfully employed and reasonably financially self-sufficient is considered to be included in what most sociologists refer to as 'the middle class' of the United States.

A person who has never attended college, does not have any specific skill, talent, or vocational training, and generally tends to work in jobs that pay a salary that is near minimum wage or barely exceeds minimum wage – as well as those who have served a significant amount of time in prison for violent crimes – are generally referred to as part of the 'lower class' of society.

A man or woman's socio-economic status or 'class' usually plays a huge part in the choice of their long-term romantic companion or future spouse. Generally speaking, most married couples who are part of the 'upper class' or 'middle class' do not want their sons or daughters marrying someone from the 'lower class.' Most parents usually want their son or daughter to marry someone who has a similar family background as their son or daughter, a similar level of intelligence and education, and no history of being convicted of any violent crimes or felonies.

One area of secondary importance for the parents of a son who has a strong desire to get married is the perceived sexual morality of their future daughter-in-law. This attitude has always been present in society, but it became of particular importance beginning with what is known as '**The Victorian Era**.'

This period of British society, which coincided with the reign of Queen Victoria (1837 – 1901), is what ushered into a society a new attitude toward marriage and how women should present themselves to men in public and society.

Without getting too detailed or too academic, this was the period that motivated the idea that women who were culturally and socially refined and women who were virgins should be the primary candidates to be a man's wife. Especially if the man was from a family that possessed a high degree of wealth, education, influence, and social status.

If a woman was considered to be one who was promiscuous, and had frequently and willingly engaged in sexual activities with some men outside the context of marriage, she was considered to be 'unfit' for marriage and motherhood.

This is one of the primary reasons why a good number of women even in today's society tend to have an adverse reaction to being labeled 'promiscuous.' When a woman is labeled kinky and promiscuous, that is essentially the same thing as saying, 'you are not worthy of having a husband, and you are not worthy of being the mother of any man's children.'

Matter of fact, an all-white wedding dress in the 19th Century and most of the 20th Century was supposed to represent that a bride was 'sexually pure' (i.e., a virgin).

Among many in society, it was considered blasphemous for a woman who had been sexually active before marriage to wear an all-white bridal gown.

Sometimes, if a woman was identified as not being a virgin days or weeks into a marriage, the parents of the groom would seek to have the marriage annulled. Many times, the father of the groom would seek a guarantee from the father of the bride that his daughter was indeed a virgin before they would allow their son to propose marriage and proceed with the wedding.

So, in a nutshell, women tended to fall into one of two categories: those women who were deemed 'worthy' of being a man's wife and worthy of being the mother of a man's children . . . and those women who were deemed 'unfit' or 'unworthy' for either role. The women in the former group were classified as being prudish, strictly monogamy-oriented 'good girls.' The women in the latter group were categorized as 'harlot,' 'slut,' 'tramp,' 'whore,' and 'mistress' types.

These classifications began way before the 19th Century, but it was during the Victorian Era where these delineations become far more emphasized and pronounced.

Also contributing to these two very different classifications among women were the prominent theories espoused in the latter part of the 19th Century and early part of the 20th

Century by a legendary psychologist named Dr. Sigmund Freud.

Freud came up with the theory of '**The Madonna / Whore Complex**,' which asserted that the vast majority of men only wanted to marry a woman who they perceived to be a fiercely loyal, very nurturing, strictly monogamy-oriented 'good girl' type who usually possessed a lot of the same personality and maternal instincts of their mother.

Freud further asserted that those same men who suffered from this 'complex' would seek out a mistress or additional lover who was much more of a 'naughty, kinky girl' type and a highly promiscuous 'slut' type for discreet, but adulterous erotic trysts on a regular, semi-regular, or occasional basis.

When you think back to my Monogamy Island example, if all men and women were only to engage in strictly monogamous sexual relationships, there would be no need for different categories or labels for women. Similarly, if all men and women were exclusively engaging in promiscuous and/or polyamorous sex, there would also be no need to differentiate women by labeling them.

I will expand on this thought in more detail in the next two chapters. First, I will examine the different categories and labels for women; then I will examine the different categories and labels for men.

Continue reading my friend.

Chapter Five

Examining the Appeal of Prudish and Monogamy-Oriented 'Good Girls' vs. Kinky and Promiscuous 'Sluts'

If a man was asked to write down a minimum of ten names of women who he would want as a potential long-term girlfriend and/or a potential wife, and then that same man was asked to write down a minimum of ten names of women who he would like to indulge in one or more episodes of kinky non-monogamous 'casual' sex with ... and once you read both lists, you saw that there were many of the same names of women included on both lists ... this would represent a man who is non-judgmental and does not suffer from the psychological effects of Dr. Sigmund Freud's *Madonna / Whore Complex.*

Conversely, if after viewing both lists offered to you by a totally different man, you noticed that the names of the women on his list of potential long-term girlfriends & potential wives were totally different than the names on the list of women who he would ideally love to engage in at least a few episodes of short-term and/or non-monogamous sex with, then you would be able to surmise that this second man generally suffers from the effects of Dr. Freud's theoretical *Madonna / Whore Complex.*

The reality is, even in today's society there are a good number of men who view women as either honest, sincere, loyal, monogamy-oriented, and sexually conservative (i.e., what many label as prudish or semi-prudish 'good girl' types) while categorizing many other women as dishonest, disingenuous, disloyal, erotically uninhibited, and highly promiscuous (i.e., what many men and women label the kinky, promiscuous 'slut' types). I would argue that there are benefits and detriments to being perceived to be in either category.

Let's examine the women who fall into these two convenient categories.

THE MONOGAMY-ORIENTED 'GOOD GIRL' TYPES

Ever since marriage became highly promoted and accepted in society, just about all single heterosexual women who aspired to have a man propose marriage to them wanted to gain the image and reputation as a loyal, sexually conservative, and monogamy-oriented 'good girl' type.

When I was young, my mother and her sisters and friends told me that my mother's nickname in college was 'The Elegant Prude.' My mother told me that when she was in college, she was known among men for having an established reputation for being a woman who was saving herself for her husband sexually until marriage.

My mother was more of the 'norm' for her generation rather than the 'exception.' Most women who were brought up in the latter half of the 19th Century and first half of the 20th Century believed that if you indulged in premarital sex with any man, you would severely damage your chances of having a man who was from a middle-class or upper-class family propose marriage to you. Having a reputation for being kinky and promiscuous was considered 'dating suicide' for the vast majority of women during that era.

The activities of the 1960s and 1970s began to change that attitude. One of the factors – in addition to those factors that were already mentioned in Chapter Two – was that once a lot of these 'good girl' types got married, and were totally ready to thoroughly enjoy themselves sexually with their husbands, many of their husbands had a very unenthusiastic reaction to it.

You see, the problem with men who suffer from Freud's *Madonna / Whore Complex* is that they do not want their wife to exhibit behavior that is in any way kinky, sexually adventurous, or polyamorous at all. These men want their wife to forever be their personal 'good girl' and 'trophy wife.' For most men who suffer from the *Madonna / Whore Complex*, the emphasis with marriage was finding a woman who would look good on their shoulders at classy social events, and who would be an exceptional mother for their children.

Dr. Freud asserted that most men do not view their mothers as sexual human beings. Most men cringe at the very idea of their mothers engaging in sexual activity. This is why a lot of men are totally against marrying a woman with a history of promiscuous behavior. It is not that men who suffer from the *Madonna / Whore Complex* 'hate' promiscuous women (for strictly sexual purposes, they love promiscuous women), but if these men happen to have one or more sons, they do not want their son(s) to view their mother as a 'slut' or 'whore' type. They feel that would deeply traumatize the psyche of their son(s).

Women, generally speaking, tend to be different. Most women have no problem accepting the fact that their mothers or fathers are very sexual in nature. Many women grow up knowing that their father may have been a womanizer type or a popular ladies' man. So for women, the sexuality of their parents is no big deal to them.

Also, when it comes to long-term relationships and marriage, men value **loyalty** more than anything. This is even true regarding men's long-term friendships with other men. Men by nature do not like to maintain long-term relationships or friendships with people who they perceive to be disloyal or undependable. They see no point.

That being the case, if a woman is promiscuous, men automatically associate that with them being disloyal. For a man, there is no point in him being in a long-term relationship with a woman if he perceives her as being disloyal. A disloyal woman is not 'wife material' in the eyes of most men.

So, what many married men do is find a woman who is a combination of loyal and monogamy-oriented to be their wife and mother to their children, and they look to find women who are very kinky and very promiscuous to indulge in extramarital affairs and erotic trysts with behind their wife's back.

In this scenario, they experience the best of both types of women. In this situation, men have sex with their wives for procreation (i.e., the conception of children) and sex with their mistresses and on-the-side lovers for recreation (i.e., the pure enjoyment of engaging in sex just for the sake of experiencing a pleasurable orgasm).

The problem with this scenario for the married women who are 'good girl' types is that they are often left feeling sexually undesirable as well as sexually frustrated because of their husband's lack of attention to their desire for sexual satisfaction. In many cases, these sexually frustrated wives will begin looking to indulge in extramarital affairs and erotic trysts of their own with men other than their husbands out of spite toward their philandering husbands.

THE KINKY PROMISCUOUS 'SLUT' TYPES

In today's society, one of the biggest issues among hardcore feminists is their harsh criticisms and rants against the notion of 'slut-shaming.' Many women in today's society, just like women in the 1950s and 1960s, do not feel that they receive the same level of personal and social respect in society if they possess a high degree of promiscuous and/or polyamorous tendencies compared to those women who are better known for being more prudish and marriage-oriented and monogamy-oriented 'good girl' types.

Many women feel that just because they want to enjoy sex outside the context of marriage, before marriage, and/or with multiple male partners does not necessarily mean that they should be treated like a 'second class citizen' or be viewed as if they are 'unworthy' of being a man's wife or the mother of his children. The truth is, they are correct in their assessment.

There is a clear 'double standard' in society between men and women when it comes to the issue of being promiscuous, polyamorous, and engaging in sex before marriage.

Men have never been viewed as being 'unworthy' of being a woman's husband or 'unfit' to be the father of her children if they engaged in sexual activities with multiple partners before marriage. If anything, men are almost **expected** to be 'sexually experienced' with many women before marriage. For many men, being a virgin on their wedding day is considered more of a 'shameful' label than a label of pride. In today's society, if it is known that a man is still a virgin past the age of 17 or 18, his male friends will usually tease him and criticize him mercilessly until he loses his virginity.

I once wrote a freelance article for an online dating advice column I maintained where I asserted that this was one of the more underrated factors that fueled the Second Wave of Feminism in the 1960s and early 1970s.

My argument was, and still is, that the latter half of the 19th Century and first half of the 20th Century led to two factions of women that were left feeling very angry, frustrated, and bitter:

1. One group, as mentioned, was what I referred to in my article as 'The Frustrated Wives.' These were women who were tired of only engaging in sex with their husbands for the purpose of producing children, and not for the sake of enjoyment and satisfaction. Secondly, these frustrated married women were tired of their husbands cheating on them with women who had a kinkier and more promiscuous nature about them. This caused the sexually frustrated wives to develop a very bitter attitude toward their husbands' many mistresses;

2. The second group was what I referred to as 'The Frustrated Mistresses.' The primary frustration by this group was that they did not receive the same level of personal and social respect in society as the 'good girl' types, and were often classified as being 'unworthy' of being a man's wife and the mother of his children. Financially, the women in this group often struggled before the 1960s because it was not easy for a woman to gain employment that would allow them to become financially self-sufficient.

Both groups of women wanted a better life for themselves, and this heavily contributed to the motivations behind the Second Wave of Feminism as well as the Sexual Liberation Movement (or 'Sexual Revolution'). Once women were able to gain decent wage-earning employment opportunities for themselves, they no longer had to rely solely on the income and financial assistance and support of men to support their desired lifestyle. The Second Wave of Feminism most benefited 'The Frustrated Mistresses' group and the Sexual Revolution / Sexual Liberation Movement most benefited 'The Frustrated Wives' group.

Women could now choose to divorce a cheating husband, or even avoid or delay getting married altogether if that is what they wanted to do. Women could also choose to give birth to a son and/or daughter without the benefit of being married or feeling obligated to have a husband in their household to help them raise a son and/or daughter.

This type of financial freedom combined with a newfound sense of sexual freedom left married women, divorced women, and unmarried women feeling empowered. Men could no longer easily 'have their cake and eat it too' (i.e., maintain a happy marriage with their wife and secretly indulge in some extramarital affairs and erotic trysts with kinky, promiscuous women on the side). The result of both the Second Wave of Feminism and the Sexual Revolution left a lot of men in society incredibly frustrated with the newly modified relationships with women. Many men did not like this new sense of 'independence' that women were experiencing.

WHOLESOME PRETENDERS
& EROTIC HYPOCRITES

If you are a man reading this paperback, and you have been a bit naïve about women up to this point (and even more so, you have never read any of my other books or listened to any of my audiobooks), then I am about to enlighten you.

If a woman is willing to be upfront and straightforwardly honest with each and every man that she meets regarding the fact that she is indeed a woman who is kinky, and a woman who has promiscuous and/or polyamorous tendencies, then those men who are primarily interested in a few episodes of short-term and/or non-monogamous 'casual' sex would immediately know what type of woman they were dealing with and they would react and respond accordingly.

Similarly, if a woman is willing to maintain a high degree of prudishness or semi-prudishness regarding her manner of sexual expression, and this woman's behavior and reputation in society can regularly confirm and support the fact that she is a woman who is strictly monogamy-oriented when it comes to engaging in sexual activities with a man, then those men who are in the market for a new long-term girlfriend and/or future wife who they very much want to remain faithfully monogamous to them would know exactly the type of women they were dealing with . . . and they would react and respond accordingly.

What if a woman who was in the 'kinky & promiscuous' category really wanted to get married? Even more specifically, what if she wanted a man to propose marriage to her who she already knew ahead of time was a very judgmental type, but she did not really care because of the fact that he was earning lots and lots of money and would promise to take care of her financially *if he was under the mistaken belief* that she was a loyal, conservative, strictly monogamy-oriented 'good girl' type? What if this woman simply wanted to experience the 'best of both worlds' and 'have her cake and eat it too' like so many men in history have done for centuries?

Enter what I have referred to for years as **Wholesome Pretenders** and **Erotic Hypocrites**.

Men have been deceitful and sexually duplicitous with women for as long as marriage has been in existence, and in the last few decades, now women feel like it is their turn to experience how that feels.

What is sexual duplicity?

As mentioned already, when a man behaves toward his wife in one manner, but when he is with one of his mistresses he behaves totally differently, this will represent a man who is **sexually duplicitous**.

For example, if a man behaves like a monogamy-oriented church-going man who frowns on the idea of pornography when he is in the company of his wife, but when he is with one of his mistresses, he regularly watches porn videos with her and uses all sorts of profanity and XXX-rated language, this would represent a man who is both *deceitful* and *duplicitous*.

I used to be this way before I began exhibiting what I now refer to as **Mode One** Behavior. Whenever I was around the women who I perceived to be 'good girl' types, I would behave differently than I did when I was around the women who I perceived to be more of a kinky and promiscuous types.

The reality is, a high percentage of women in society are **just like this**. So, what women who are *Wholesome Pretenders* & *Erotic Hypocrites* do is, they behave like a prudish and monogamy-oriented 'good girl' type when they are around men who they want to earn a marriage proposal from, or at minimum, from men who they want to treat them with the highest degree of personal and social respect ... but then, when they are around men who they know are kinky, erotically dominant, and exceptional in bed, they will quickly reveal their more free-spirited and erotically uninhibited side.

In my other books, I even introduce a fourth category of women: women who will blatantly lead a man into believing that he will 'one day soon' gain the opportunity to engage in sexual activities with them, but in reality, these women have no real intentions of allowing those men to have sex with them. I refer to these women as *Manipulative Timewasters* (Note: My book, *The Possibility of Sex* goes into more detail about the *Manipulative Timewaster* types).

Understand this about women: the vast majority of women only want a man's companionship for **three primary reasons** and those three reasons are:

- **Enjoyable and satisfying sex;**
- **Entertaining conversation & enjoyable social companionship;**
- **Financial assistance and support and/or non-financial assistance and support from a man to help them raise one or more children;**

Some women might want to spend time with a man for just one of those three reasons only. Other women might want to spend time with men for two of those three reasons. Many other women might want to spend time with a man for **all three reasons**. It just depends on the woman, and what she feels that particular man has to offer.

Here would be what I categorize as the four types of men that all women want to interact with for one or more of those three primary reasons above:

Category #1: Men who women want to spend time with solely and specifically for the purpose of sexual enjoyment and satisfaction;

Category #2: Men who women want to spend time with primarily for sexual enjoyment and satisfaction, as well as a small degree of financial and/or non-financial assistance and support and enjoyable & entertaining non-sexual social companionship;

Category #3: Men who women want to spend time with primarily for financial and/or non-financial assistance and support, as well a small degree of sexual companionship and enjoyable & entertaining non-sexual social companionship;

Category #4: Men who women want to spend time with strictly for enjoyable & entertaining non-sexual companionship;

I refer to the men in Category #1 as *Total Alpha males*, the men in Category #2 as *Alpha males with a few Beta traits and tendencies*, the men in Category #3 as *Beta males with a few Alpha traits and tendencies*, and the men in Category #4 as *Total Beta males*.

I will discuss each of the men in these four categories in my very next chapter.

Continue reading my friend.

Chapter Six

The Roles that Alpha Males and Beta Males Fulfill for Women

Many dating and relationships advice books have highlighted how different men and women are physically, mentally, and emotionally. The list of differences is too long to repeat.

What many men and women tend to overlook and underestimate is just how **similar** men and women are in various ways. For example, I have pointed out in my previous books that both men and women have fears and insecurities that negatively affect their behavior. Members of both genders tend to engage in their share of 'manipulative head games' with one another.

As I just mentioned in the previous chapter, one characteristic about women that many men tend to be naïve and even ignorant about is the fact that **women can be just as sexually duplicitous as men can be**.

Women have their version of loyal and monogamy-oriented 'good guys' and promiscuous and/or polyamorous 'kinky sluts.' Women usually refer to the 'good guy' types as 'nice guys' or 'gentlemen.' On the other hand, women usually refer to the kinkier, erotically dominant, and promiscuous types as 'bad boys' or 'womanizers.'

In the MANosphere, we refer to these two types as 'Alpha' males and 'Beta' males.

Remember my Preface chapter? When I used the example of Kevin and Tyrone? In my examples on the fictional Monogamy Island, the fictional character of Kevin represented the prototypical 'Beta' male while the fictional character of Tyrone represented the typical 'Alpha' male.

In the real world, Kevin would have possessed much more wealth and far more material assets than he did, and Tyrone would have been far more promiscuous than he was in my scenario. That aside, you got the gist of each while reading the Preface.

Instead of only two categories, I tend to place all heterosexual men into four categories as I mentioned in the previous chapter: *Total Alpha males, Alpha males with a few Beta traits and tendencies, Beta males with a few Alpha traits and tendencies*, and *Total Beta males*. I will discuss the general characteristics of each archetype in this chapter.

THE TOTAL ALPHA MALE

A man who is a *Total Alpha male* is perceived by women in the same manner that most men view a woman who is a kinky, highly promiscuous 'slut' type. You could nickname *Total Alpha male* types as 'male-sluts' or 'man-whores.' A more common term is 'prolific and incorrigible womanizers.'

Very few women want a *Total Alpha male* as their long-term boyfriend or husband. Particularly if that woman is very monogamy-oriented, or at least, 'pretends to be' in public.

Total Alpha males are women's 'secret guilty pleasure.' These are the type of men who married women will cheat with behind their husband's back. Similarly, unmarried women will engage in sex that is much kinkier with a *Total Alpha male* than they will with a man who is their long-term romantic boyfriend.

Men who are *Total Alpha males* rarely divide women into the categories of 'good girls' and 'sluts.' In the mind of a *Total Alpha male*, **ALL WOMEN** have the potential to become a kinky and promiscuous or polyamorous sex partner for them. *Total Alpha males* do not believe any woman is as 'innocent,' 'prudish,' and/or as 'monogamy-oriented' as they pretend to be in public.

Most men who were street pimps in the 1970s and 1980s were *Total Alpha male* types. These men possessed so much confidence, so much charisma, and so much seductive charm and sexual prowess that they always had more than their fair share of women offering them invitations to engage in sexual activities with them.

Instead of simply having sex with all of these women, what pimps did is essentially 'loan out' their lovers to men who fell into the other three archetype categories, and they profited from it.

The street pimp profited from the *Alpha male with a few Beta traits and tendencies* types because many men in this category were sexually duplicitous and adulterous types that would be looking to cheat on their wife on a regular, semi-regular, or occasional basis. So, men of this type would use the services provided by a street pimp and his stable of whores.

The street pimp profited from the *Beta male with a few Alpha traits and tendencies* types because many men in this category who were married would be denied sex by their wives sometimes for days, weeks, or even months ... and if they were unmarried, they just did not have the social skills and seductive charm needed to persuade women to engage in short-term non-monogamous 'casual' sex with them. So, they would pay for the services provided by a street pimp and his stable of whores.

Finally, the street pimp very much profited from the *Total Beta male* types because men in this category had no 'game' or seductive charm with women at all. These were the men who were considered 'chumps' and 'losers' when it came to socially interacting with women. So, these men would gladly pay for the services provided by a street pimp and his stable of whores.

Men who are *Total Alpha male* types tend to be highly self-assured, kinky, extremely erotically dominant with women, and very skilled when it comes to seducing a woman into having sex with them as well as usually leaving those women feeling very pleased and satisfied sexually. Women naturally gravitate to these men when they are feeling horny for wild, kinky type sex.

Not too many men who are born with a 'silver spoon in their mouth' grow up to become *Total Alpha male* types. Men in this category typically are men who have had to compete for everything they have achieved in their life, and they have developed an ultra-strong sense of backbone and resilience along the way to survive and overcome their episodes of adversity. These men are anything but coddled 'mama's boy' types. These are real men with a high degree of masculinity.

Men in this category are loved and respected by women because they are not afraid to speak their mind, and they could care less what other people say negatively about them behind their back. They know who they are, and they know what they need to do to get what they want out of life, and that is all they care about. Figuratively speaking (and sometimes literally), these men have the 'biggest pair of balls' of any of the men from the other three categories. Nothing cowardly about them.

Total Alpha male types don't 'beat-around-the-bush' with women. They let women know upfront and straightforwardly that their primary reason for socially interacting with a woman is for the purpose of engaging in sexual activity. Men in this category are very open and public about the fact that they possess a high degree of promiscuous and polyamorous tendencies.

Many women who normally do not indulge in short-term and/or non-monogamous 'casual' sex will many times do so with a *Total Alpha male* type. Most women know these men are not ever going to commit to them in a 'boyfriend-girlfriend' type relationship or a strictly monogamous marriage. Women are realistic in this regard. Again, women who connect with *Total Alpha male* types are those who are looking solely and specifically to be seduced into engaging in a few episodes of short-term and/or non-monogamous 'casual' sex, and these women are expecting to be pleased and thoroughly satisfied in bed once they agree to have sex with a *Total Alpha male* type.

You will rarely if ever catch a man who is a *Total Alpha male* type raping women or date-raping women. They simply have no reason to. Women constantly throw themselves at men in this category. Many times, men in this category have to reject and decline invitations from women to engage in sex.

The problems and weaknesses of men who are Total Alpha male types are that they have to be able to defend themselves against other men who become envious and jealous of their sexual popularity with women. For example, a lot of 'jealous husband' types and 'jealous boyfriend' types will often come after a *Total Alpha male* type looking for a measure of revenge once they find out that a *Total Alpha male* has been seducing and having sex with their wife, fiancée, or long-term girlfriend.

Many men who are *Total Alpha male* types tend to have problems maintaining '9-to-5' type jobs because they do not like taking orders from a 'boss' or 'supervisor.' Men in this category tend to do better for themselves when they are self-employed and answer to no one.

Consequently, *Total Alpha male* types often end up being erratically employed and full of financial struggles from time to time. Many *Total Alpha male* types, if they are between 18 and

35, will have older women who act as 'Sugar Mamas' for them, and those women will perform some financial favors for them to prevent them from having too many financial problems.

If there is one type of woman that *Total Alpha male* types sometimes tend to miss out on connecting with, it would be women who are deeply religious and full of conviction about only indulging in strictly monogamy-oriented sex.

Also, because of their dominant and uncompromising nature, many women shy away from spending time with men in this category in any sort of non-sexual manner, and this is totally fine with *Total Alpha male* types. Men who are *Total Alpha male* types do not enjoy being around women in a non-physical or non-sexual manner.

Total Alpha male types will usually only interact with women non-sexually for business-related purposes or to receive some money from women. *Total Alpha male* types will rarely elect to spend 'quality time' with a woman in a non-physical, non-sexual, purely platonic manner on a regular basis. That is simply not in their DNA to do so. Also, a *Total Alpha male* type will typically not allow a woman to get away with behavior that he perceives to be disrespectful, spoiled or highly argumentative.

Many times, *Total Alpha male* types do not even like to raise children. Quite often after impregnating a woman, they will simply take off ... never to be heard from again (what women and the U.S. judicial system refers to as 'deadbeat dads'). It is rare when a Total Alpha male type intentionally seeks to get a woman pregnant unless he is roughly 36 years of age or older, and he has finally decided to make an effort to settle down with just one woman. But if that is the case, he will no longer be able to be truly categorized as a *Total Alpha male.* That would mean this man has reached a point where he is ready to transition into being an *Alpha male with a few Beta traits and tendencies.*

THE ALPHA MALE with a few BETA traits and tendencies

There are two categories of men who are not exclusively Alpha males nor Beta males. They are more so a 'blend' of both.

The first of these two categories I will discuss is what I refer to as an *Alpha male with a few Beta traits and tendencies.* Men in this category usually fall into one of two categories: **1)** Men who used to be *Total Alpha male* types, but as they got older, they found themselves becoming more relationship and family oriented, as well as they transitioned into becoming a bit more friendly, more personable, and easier to get along with in one-on-one social situations ... or ... **2)** Men who used to be either a *Beta male with a few Alpha traits and tendencies* type or a *Total Beta male* type who might have lost a significant amount of weight (if previously fat or obese), gained some weight (in the form of muscle, if they were previously skinny), improved degree of seductive charm and overall sex appeal, significantly improved their sense of confidence and backbone, significantly improved their overall conversation skills and social skills, and most importantly ... improved their 'bedroom game' and overall sexual prowess.

Here is the rather 'sneaky' thing about many men in this category: Remember when I said that men who are *Total Alpha male* types will typically 'miss out' on connecting with the women who are deeply religious and totally committed to only indulging in sex with men within the context of a strictly monogamous relationship or marriage? Well, that is where the typical sexual duplicity of men in this category comes in. You could say, many men in this category are the male equivalent to a *Wholesome Pretender* type. They will behave in a very 'gentlemanly' type manner around women who they know are a bit prudish and very monogamy-oriented, but then when they are around women who are kinkier and more promiscuous, they will behave just like a *Total Alpha male* type would.

Women who are very monogamy-oriented but also very feminine and submissive in nature always tend to gravitate toward the *Alpha male with a few Beta traits and tendencies*. They see these men as 'real men' who will also remain faithfully monogamous and financially responsible throughout the entire course of their relationship and marriage.

Women who are kinkier and more promiscuous also want to connect with men in this category because men in this category tend to possess a high degree of persuasive and seductive charm with women.

The major weakness of men in this category is simply that they are the most like to cheat on their long-time girlfriends and commit adultery while married. With the exception of some of the older members of this category who feel like they have already sowed as many 'wild oats' as humanly possible in their younger years, most men in this category find it extremely challenging to remain faithfully monogamous to just one woman forever. Men in this category usually have too many options.

Many men in this category will eventually succumb to the temptation of quick, easy sex offered to them by potential mistress and on-the-side lover types. If they get caught, they end up being branded as a cheater or an adulterer, and then many women lose a measure of respect for them and their popularity with women begins to diminish slowly. Their reputation becomes tarnished. No longer are they viewed as the 'good catch' they once were.

At the risk of generalizing, a good number of men who are Entertainment Industry celebrities, professional athletes, and popular politicians tend to fall into the category of an *Alpha male with a few Beta traits and tendencies*. These men want to maintain the public image of being a 'monogamy-oriented gentleman,' but behind-closed-doors, they want to experience the sex life of a successful male porn star.

The men in this category who are the least likely to remain monogamous for too long are the men who formerly were Beta male types who now – because of various forms of self-improvement activities and a stronger sense of backbone – have 'upgraded' themselves to the category of an *Alpha male with a few Beta traits and tendencies*. These men have never really received invitations to engage in 'casual sex' with women before, so that becomes very exciting to them, and most of the time, the temptation is just too much for them to resist with ease.

There is one additional group of men who possess a 'blend' of both 'Alpha' and 'Beta' traits, but their characteristics lean much more toward the 'Beta' side of things than the 'Alpha' side.

THE BETA MALE with a few ALPHA traits and tendencies

There are some men who because their mother was divorced while they were young, widowed while they were young, or they happened to have been born out of wedlock and never really knew their father, they were primarily raised by their mother and their mother only. These men usually had no real strong 'father figure' in their lives while growing up, or if their father was involved in their life, the father had more of a passive type personality compared to their stronger, more domineering mother who pretty much controlled the household.

When a man is raised primarily or exclusively by his mother, step-mother, or grandmother, they are either going to 'rebel' against their parent or guardian at some point and seek the guidance of some older more masculine male mentor (this is why many men who are teenagers and young adults join street gangs) ... or ... they are going to consciously or subconsciously find themselves becoming what is known as a 'mama's boy' type who is accustomed to being heavily nurtured and coddled by the women in his life.

Many men who are raised under the heavy influence of women (mothers, step-mothers, aunts, grandmothers, older sisters, etc.) usually tend to grow up to become one of the two Beta male types (either a *Beta male with a few Alpha traits and tendencies* or a *Total Beta male*).

A lot of Beta male types are groomed by their mothers to hold women in the highest regard and always present themselves to women as a polite, respectful, accommodating 'gentleman.' They are taught at a young age that a man should always pay for dates with women and that they should suppress their sexual desires until they are married, engaged, or at least committed to being involved in a long-term monogamous 'boyfriend-girlfriend' type relationship with a woman.

The older women in their life usually brainwash them to believe that pursuing women for short-term non-monogamous 'casual' sex is something that the vast majority of women will perceive as 'disrespectful,' 'shallow,' and 'socially inappropriate.'

Women who want to maintain a high degree of control and influence over their husbands and male romantic companions gravitate to men in this category very frequently. If a man in this category possesses a college education, a high-status job, and a six figure or seven figure income, he will usually be able to find a woman to propose marriage to with relative ease.

When a man in this category meets a woman who is a virgin, or a woman who has never dated or had sex with an Alpha male type, then a man in this category will not experience too many problems with his girlfriend, fiancée, or wife. More-than-likely, these two will get along fine, get married, have a few children, and come close to living "happily ever after."

The problem emerges with men in this category when they intentionally or unintentionally connect with a woman who has a history of dating and having sex with men who are more

Alpha in nature. Realistically, once a woman has had sex repeatedly with an Alpha male type, she will always perceive a man who is a Beta male type to be boring and unsatisfying sexually.

This is why a lot of mothers and fathers who have one or more daughters do not want their daughter(s) dating an Alpha male type while they are in high school or college. The parents know the type of effect an Alpha male will have on their daughter(s) sexually, so they make every effort to paint Alpha male types as 'the bad boys' or the 'not good for you at all' types.

Once a woman gets 'turned out' by an Alpha male (i.e., makes the transition from having a prudish monogamy-oriented mindset to more of a kinky, promiscuous or polyamorous mindset), more-than-likely that woman is always going to want to share the company of an erotically dominant Alpha male for sexual enjoyment and satisfaction purposes. This has a high potential to cause major problems if a man who is a *Beta male with a few Alpha traits and tendencies* decides to marry a woman of this nature, or enter into a long-term monogamous 'boyfriend-girlfriend' type relationship with a woman of this nature.

The men who are *Beta males with a few Alpha traits and tendencies* types can fully expect to attract more than their fair share of *Wholesome Pretender & Erotic Hypocrite* types (and even quite a few *Manipulative Timewaster* types as well). Women who are materialistic gold digger types LOVE the men in this category, assuming that the man is earning six figures or higher.

The men in this category are the type of men that kinky and promiscuous women tend to generally ignore while they are in high school and college, but once they see that men in this category are now financially self-sufficient or even wealthy, then the women who are the kinky and promiscuous types know how to 'play the role' of the prudish and monogamy-oriented 'good girl' type. In other words, they very much know how to become a sexually duplicitous *Wholesome Pretender* type.

Why do so many *Wholesome Pretender & Erotic Hypocrite* types gravitate toward men who are *Beta males with a few Alpha traits and tendencies* types so much?

Two reasons:

1.   Men who are *Beta males with a few Alpha traits and tendencies* generally tend to have a natural tendency to want to fulfill the role of the 'Financial Provider' for their wives, fiancées, and girlfriends; Men in this category are usually wealthy or at minimum, very financially responsible and self-sufficient; Men in this category have arguably the highest collective net worth of men from any of the four archetypes;

2. Men who are *Beta males with a few Alpha traits and tendencies* tend to display the most flattering, entertaining, and accommodating personality traits as well as the most monogamy-oriented and family-oriented behavior compared to Alpha male types. Men in this category usually have been raised and groomed by older women to always display the highest level of personal and social respect toward women;

The sad aspect for men in this category is that they will usually be cheated on by women more than any Alpha male ever will. Once again, women who are used to having sex with Alpha male types will never be indefinitely faithful to a Beta male type. Never. The only women who will ever be indefinitely loyal and faithfully monogamous to a Beta male type will be a woman who is a virgin, or a woman who has never engaged in sexual activities with an erotically dominant Alpha male type.

The only instances when men in this category will be perceived as being more 'Alpha' than 'Beta' is when they feel they have been disrespected, humiliated, or exploited by a woman. When a man in this category reaches a 'boiling point' of anger and frustration, their sense of backbone will suddenly emerge, and they will not allow themselves to be disrespected or treated in an undesirable manner any longer. Many married men in this category tend to gain a reputation for being 'passive-aggressive' and can even be known to initiate acts of domestic violence and physical abuse toward women.

It is the complaints, frustrations, and overall jaded attitudes expressed by men in this category (either to me individually or in the MANosphere in general) that most contributed to my motivation to writing this particular paperback.

There is only one category of men who have it worse than a *Beta male with a few Alpha traits and tendencies*, and that is what I refer to as a *Total Beta male*.

THE TOTAL BETA MALE

There are three types of men that those in the MANosphere tend to criticize mercilessly, tease, and disparage:

- **'Incel'** types (short for 'involuntarily celibate')
- **'White Knight'** types
- **'Captain Save-a-Ho'** types

The term 'incel' represents a man whose social skills are so underdeveloped, and he lacks so much confidence and anything resembling adequate attraction and seduction skills with women that he finds himself 'involuntarily celibate' for months, years, and sometimes even decades. These men are often referred to by other men as being 'total losers' with women.

A 'White Knight' is a man who will go out of his way to defend women anytime various aspects of their behavior are harshly criticized by men or other women. These are men who firmly believe that women do not possess any 'unappealing qualities' or any major flaws and weaknesses in their character or behavior, and these men believe ALL women are worthy of being deemed a 'good girl' or a 'goddess' who is deserving of being any man's girlfriend, fiancée, and/or wife.

A 'Captain Save-a-Ho' is very similar to a 'White Knight' type, with the only difference being that they will treat a 'slut' type or a materialistic and promiscuous 'whore' type with the same level of respect and kindness that other men would only offer to a prudish and monogamy-oriented 'good girl' type. These are men who are naïve enough to believe that if they show a highly promiscuous woman enough love and respect, that these women will become so grateful that they will suddenly develop a desire to enter into a long-term, strictly monogamous romantic relationship or marriage with them. Bless their hearts.

Women love to recruit men who are *Total Beta male* types to be their 'play brother' or 'male girlfriend.' Women love to spend time with men in this category for purely platonic purposes and to engage in trivial but entertaining gossip. Women love to vent with men in this category about the disappointments and frustrations they have experienced after dating or having sex with Alpha male types. They feel men who are *Total Beta males* tend to make great 'empathetic listening ear' types.

Other men in the *Total Beta male* category, either because of some form of mental illness or maybe even autism or some other social communication disorder, tend to have such underdeveloped social skills that they tend to be perceived by women as being 'weird' or 'creepy' which causes many women to avoid any form of social interactions with them altogether.

The men in this category who are completely and indefinitely ignored by women, or treated like nothing more than a 'purely platonic friend' for their entire adult life causes a lot of men in this category to eventually become anti-social, and it causes them to develop a high degree of misogynistic bitterness toward women over a period of years and decades as they get older.

Plain and simple, no heterosexual man wants to remain in this category indefinitely. The best sex life any man can hope for if he is in this category is either **a)** spending money on the services provided by street prostitutes, professional Call Girls, or upscale Erotic Escorts, or **b)** masturbating to internet porn on a week-to-week, month-to-month, year-to-year basis.

In worst case scenario, some men in this category end up committing suicide. They reach a point where they feel life is simply not worth living if they cannot attract the romantic and sexual attention & companionship of any woman at all. There have been a few cases in the 21st Century where men in this category have gone as far as to commit a murder-suicide, where they will target and murder womanizing Alpha males, the women who gravitate toward those Alpha males, before finally killing themselves rather than spend the rest of their lives in prison.

A lot of times, men who used to be in the category of a *Beta male with a few Alpha traits and tendencies* tend to fall into this category if they become morbidly obese, lose their job and remain unemployed for a long stretch of time, or they become completely broke or bankrupt because of bad financial decisions and poor investments. Many men in this category sometimes tend to suffer from alcohol and/or drug abuse, and many of them battle with bouts of depression later in life.

Here is how I would evaluate my four archetypes of men:

My rating for **Total Alpha male** types on a 5-star rating scale:

Enjoyable and Satisfying Sex for women: **4 or 5 stars**
Entertaining Conversation and Enjoyable Social Companionship: **1 star**
Financial or Non-Financial Assistance & Support as well as Emotional Empathy and Support for women: **1 or 2 stars**

Defining Characteristic: Even when the men in this category refuse to spend money on women, and refuse to promise women any long-term monogamy (causing many women to refer to these men as 'jerks' and other similar labels), these men are still able to attract, seduce, and engage in sexual activities with a high number of women on a regular basis

My rating for **Alpha male with a few Beta traits and tendencies** types on a 5-star rating scale:

Enjoyable and Satisfying Sex for women: **3 or 4 stars**

Entertaining Conversation and Enjoyable Social Companionship: **2 or 3 stars**

Financial or Non-Financial Assistance & Support as well as Emotional Empathy and Support for women: **3 or 4 stars**

Defining Characteristic: Men in this category are the most likely to cheat on their long-term girlfriends or commit adultery when they are married; Men in this category are typically very sexually duplicitous, and know how to behave like the 'perfect gentleman' around women who they perceive to be prudish and monogamy-oriented, but will behave more like a Total Alpha male type when they are around women who they perceive to be kinkier and more promiscuous

My rating for **_Beta male with a few Alpha traits and tendencies types_** on a 5-star rating scale:

Enjoyable and Satisfying Sex for women: **2 or 3 stars**

Entertaining Conversation and Enjoyable Social Companionship: **3 or 4 stars**

Financial or Non-Financial Assistance & Support as well as Emotional Empathy and Support for women: **4 or 5 stars**

Defining Characteristic: Men in this category are generally only able to attract the romantic and/or sexual attention & companionship of women when they possess a very flattering, accommodating, and entertaining personality, a high degree of fame and/or social status, and most importantly a high degree of income and wealth and a reputation for being extremely financially generous with women and financially supportive of women by offering them an affluent, high quality lifestyle; Once you take away their finances and their willingness to offer women some degree of financial assistance and support, women will begin to treat them as nothing more than a 'purely platonic friend' type rather than a boyfriend or husband type

<u>My rating for **_Total Beta male_** types on a 5-star rating scale</u>:

Enjoyable and Satisfying Sex for women: **1 star**
Entertaining Conversation and Enjoyable Social Companionship: **4 or 5 stars**
Financial or Non-Financial Assistance & Support as well as Emotional Empathy and Support for women: **2 or 3 stars**

Defining Characteristic: Even when men in this category offer to spend money on women and offer to promise women indefinite monogamy, women still are only willing to treat them as nothing more than a 'purely platonic friend' type; sometimes, men in this category are completely and indefinitely ignored by women and/or perceived by women to be 'weird' or 'creepy' if they have severely underdeveloped social skills

Bottom line is this:

Women gravitate toward Alpha male types primarily for their sexual attention and companionship, and they gravitate toward Beta male types when their interests lean more toward receiving non-sexual attention and companionship from men as well as receiving financial assistance and support from men.

If all of the prudish and strictly monogamy-oriented women of the world were only interested in dating the Beta males of society ... and all of the kinky and promiscuous and/or polyamorous women only gravitated toward the Alpha males of society ... then this is when dating and relationships would be easy. There would be very few problems, very few misunderstandings, very few arguments, no cheating or adultery, and sadly ... no demand for professional dating coaches and polyamory advisors such as myself (my career would be over).

The good news for me is that I still have a job, and the reason I still have a job is because realistically, you are always going to have men who are going to behave in a deceitful, manipulative, and/or sexually duplicitous manner toward women, and you are always going to have a good number of women who are going to exhibit the same characteristics with men.

Women who are sexually duplicitous want **both types** of men in their life. They want the Alpha males primarily for sexual enjoyment and satisfaction, and they want the Beta males primarily for platonic companionship and financial assistance & support.

Men who are sexually duplicitous also want **both types** of women in their life. They want the loyal, prudish, and monogamy-oriented 'good girl' types for long-term relationships and marriage, and they want the kinky and promiscuous 'slut' types for short-term and/or non-monogamous 'casual' sex.

Yes, there is a small percentage of men who only want to connect with prudish and monogamy-oriented types (usually Beta males) as well as a small percentage of men who only want to connect with kinky and promiscuous or polyamorous types (usually *Total Alpha male* types). A larger percentage want both types in their life.

Similarly, there is a small percentage of women who only want to interact exclusively with Alpha males, and another small percentage of women who only want to be in a relationship with Beta males, but a larger percentage of women want 'one of each' in their life.

In the very next chapter, I will go into more detail about how the knowledge, wisdom, and general advice offered by the MANosphere has contributed to many men's desire to transform themselves from maintaining a 'Beta male' oriented mindset to developing more of a highly masculine, take-no-crap-from-women 'Alpha male' type mentality toward interacting with women romantically, sexually, and socially.

Continue reading my friend.

Chapter Seven

The Emergence of 'The Beta Male Revolution'

Let's say, starting with 1866 thru roughly 1959, here is how things were going with the men in the four categories mentioned in Chapter Six:

- *Total Alpha male* types were either unmarried and messing around with nothing but the few openly kinky and promiscuous type women ... or those who were married had wives who allowed them to take on one or more mistresses as long as those mistresses were respectful and deferential to the wives and did not cause any problems;

- *Alpha males with a few Beta traits and tendencies* types were either happily married with children, or still dating and searching for their wife to be; as time went on, these men began to become more deceitful and sexually duplicitous, and they began cheating on their wife behind her back;

- *Beta males with a few Alpha traits and tendencies* types were considered the 'good men' of society who always remained faithfully monogamous to their wives and did everything within their power to raise good children and provide for their family;

- *Total Beta male* types were also usually able to connect with a woman and get married and have children, even though they may have had to work two or three jobs to make ends meet; a few men in this category were not able to connect with a woman and get married because of various issues (e.g., mental illness, personality disorders, chronically unemployed, etc.)

If I had to point the finger at the one category of men who angered women so much that it contributed to the objectives of the Second Wave of Feminism, it was the *Alpha males with a few Beta traits and tendencies* types (and to a far lesser extent, the *Total Alpha male* types).

Many women respected the *Total Alpha male* types because even though they experienced the best of both worlds, at least they were **upfront and straightforwardly honest** with their wives about it. There was no deceit or duplicity going on.

On the other hand, with the men who were *Alpha males with a few Beta traits and tendencies* types, women felt totally betrayed and heartbroken. Of the four categories of men, it was these men who were viewed as the 'bad guys' of dating and relationships, and marriage.

Then, the 1960s and 1970s changed all of that. Well, sort of. Let's look at how things changed for the men in each category beginning with roughly 1980:

- Not too much has changed with the *Total Alpha male* types. Many of them are still unmarried and having sex with women who are either openly kinky and promiscuous, or, they are having sex with women who are *Wholesome Pretender & Erotic Hypocrite* types. And If they happen to be married, their wives allow them to have sex with additional lovers as long as those mistresses are respectful and deferential to the wives and do not cause any problems;

- Similarly, not all that much has changed with the *Alpha males with a few Beta traits and tendencies* types either. Most men in this category are either happily married with children or still dating and searching for their wife to be. A good number of them are still exhibiting behavior that is deceitful and sexually duplicitous, and they are cheating on their wife behind her back on a regular, semi-regular, or occasional basis;

- Because of feminism and the Sexual Revolution, many women who were previously attracted to the *Beta males with a few Alpha traits and tendencies* now find themselves gravitating (intentionally or unintentionally) to more Alpha male types. Many women who are *Wholesome Pretender & Erotic Hypocrite types* as well as materialistic 'gold digger' types now gravitate to men in this category for marriage and long-term relationships, but usually unbeknownst to their boyfriends or husbands, these same types of women are now cheating on men in this category behind-their-back with Alpha males;

- *Total Beta male* types are now being left in the dust. Men in this category will only be able to attract a girlfriend or wife if they are in a social environment where money is not an issue, and everyone is committed to strict monogamy. Realistically, in the world we live in now, that is simply not the case. These days, women do nothing but 'use' men in this category for their flattering and accommodating personalities and their emotional empathy and support.

In a nutshell, Beta males are the ones being shafted.

The *Beta males with a few Alpha traits and tendencies* types do not feel like they can completely trust women anymore. They feel most women who seek to connect with them want to just 'use' them for their financial resources and willingness to spend time with them non-sexually, but those women do not truly love them (think about the fictional character of Kevin on Monogamy Island in the Preface Chapter).

At minimum, the men who are *Beta males with a few Alpha traits and tendencies* feel like they are now the men that many women turn to only after these women have "sowed their wild oats" with a high number of Alpha male types.

For the *Total Beta male* types, things are even worse. The men in this category are almost completely shunned by women when it comes to romance and sex.

If a *Total Beta male* type is not willing to function as a woman's 'play brother' or 'male girlfriend,' women want nothing to do with them. Especially if these men are broke, unemployed, or have major personality issues and underdeveloped social skills.

Again, the men who should be paying the price of feminism right now should be the men who are the *Alpha males with a few Beta traits and tendencies types*. Most Beta males feel like those deceitful and sexually duplicitous Alpha male types should be the ones who women should be ignoring indefinitely and choosing not to have anything to do with romantically or sexually. In an ideal world, things probably would have worked out like that. Sadly, this is not an ideal world.

As of right now, society has three categories of men and women:

- Men and women who are only into strict monogamy
- Men and women who are openly promiscuous and/or polyamorous
- Men and women who are deceitfully promiscuous and/or polyamorous

Obviously, the men and women in that last category are causing all of the problems, disappointments, frustrations, and heartbreak. Finding out exactly how to identify the men and women in that last category was essentially what caused the dating advice industry to explode beginning with the early 2000s.

Men who now fully realize that they are perceived by most women as being more 'Beta' than 'Alpha' are reading more blogs and books than ever before, they are listening to more podcast programs than ever before, and they are attending more PUA bootcamps, manhood-oriented and masculinity-oriented workshops, and men's conferences that center on the attraction and seduction of women than at any time in this nation's history.

Welcome to what I frequently refer to as **The Beta Male Revolution**. *Sometimes things have to get worse before they get better, and this definitely applies to today's dating scene that involves heterosexual dating singles.* The Beta Male Revolution is Beta males' answer to the Second Wave of Feminism and the Sexual Revolution of the 1960s and 1970s.

Beginning with no later than 2001, many Alpha male types have even been helping fuel this Beta Male Revolution. In the same way street pimps (a.k.a. *Total Alpha male* types) found a way to earn a profit for themselves by 'loaning out' their casual sex lovers to Beta male types for a fee in the 1970s and 1980s, many Alpha male types in the 21st Century are not simply giving Beta male types some 'fish' ... but instead, they are teaching Beta males **how to catch their own 'fish'** (in other words, PUAs and similar types are not interested in 'matchmaking' or 'pimping' ... they would rather teach Beta male types how to attract, charm, and seduce women themselves).

Enter the Attraction & Seduction Industry, or what is also known simply as 'The Pickup Artist Community' or 'The Seduction Community.'

I earn my living by providing knowledge, wisdom, and general advice to men ... and I would easily say that the vast majority of my male clients are Beta male types looking for advice on how to become more 'Alpha.'

I consider myself different than the average, conventional 'pickup artist' (PUA) though. Many PUA types tend to endorse a method of socially interacting with women and seducing women that is more 'indirect' as well as misleading and manipulative in nature.

What many PUA types and other 'indirect' dating coaches do is not so much encourage Beta males to become more 'Alpha,' but rather, they teach Beta males how to use their image and reputation for being a 'nice, friendly, monogamy-oriented' guy to mislead women into believing that they are interested in being a woman's next long-term boyfriend and/or future husband, but then, once the manipulative Beta male is fortunate enough to engage in sexual activities with that woman one or more times ... this man then just makes up a reason to break up with the woman and then move on to his next female target.

Obviously, this type of PUA technique will not work with a woman who is committed to practicing celibacy prior to marriage, but it works very well with women who have already been sexually active with a number of men or women who are virgins who are comfortable with the idea of losing their virginity outside the context of marriage to a man who they believe really cares for them.

This is referred to as the 'indirect' method of connecting with women for sex. This method leaves a lot of women feeling misled, manipulated, and heartbroken, but do you think Beta males really care? Of course not.

Devoted students of professional PUAs could care less about women's feelings. These men maintain the attitude that it is better to mislead and manipulate a woman for her sexual companionship than to allow yourself to be misled and manipulated by a woman for your non-sexual companionship and financial resources.

What I am known for teaching is a more 'direct' and non-manipulative method of connecting with women romantically and sexually. I believe men should simply verbally communicate to women upfront and straightforwardly that they have absolutely no interest in engaging in a series of purely platonic social interactions with women, and that they have no interest whatsoever in being groomed to become a woman's 'platonic boyfriend' and/or 'platonic husband' who provides them with nothing more than entertaining conversation and various financial favors.

I believe men should let women of interest know what their true romantic or sexual desires, interests, and intentions are in an upfront and straightforwardly honest manner, and if what is really on a man's mind is short-term and/or non-monogamous 'casual' sex, then that men should let women know this directly. I refer to this type of bold, upfront, unapologetic, straightforward honesty as **The Mode One Approach** of verbal communication.

Many men, and in particular Beta male types, have joined what is known as 'The Men's Rights Movement' and/or the MGTOW (Men Going Their Own Way) Movement. I will discuss these two movements in more detail in Part Three of this paperback.

How is all of this affecting society?

1. Total Beta male types who are categorized as 'incels' are becoming more misogynistic and more violent than ever. Pretty soon, these isolated cases of murder-suicides (or suicides only) are only going to increase;

2. Total Beta male types who were once categorized as 'White Knight' types have now begun to stop defending women on social media and blog sites and instead have turned on women and have begun verbally attacking them;

3. Total Beta male types who were once categorized as 'Captain Save-a-Ho' types have stopped attempting to pursue women with promiscuous and polyamorous tendencies for long-term romantic relationships, and they have stopped behaving like

'male girlfriends' and 'empathetic listening ears' to these women; Now, they are attempting to seduce them into engaging in one or more episodes of short-term non-monogamous 'casual sex,' and if they fail, they are cutting all ties with these women;

4. Men who are *Beta males with a few Alpha traits and tendencies* types are beginning to avoid entering into long-term monogamous romantic relationships and marriages with women who are 30 years of age or older if they suspect these women of having a history of highly promiscuous behavior with a wide assortment of Alpha male types between the ages of 15 and 29; This is causing there to be more unmarried women who are 30 years of age or older. If a woman is roughly 36 years of age or older, they will probably be completely ignored by men who are *Beta males with a few Alpha traits and tendencies* types (at least for marriage or long-term relationships).

In a nutshell, it was the Beta male types that most women who were *Wholesome Pretender* & *Erotic Hypocrite* types (i.e., the sexually duplicitous women) depended on to always treat them as if they were worthy of being a man's long-term girlfriend, fiancée, and wife. At minimum, sexually duplicitous women felt like they could bank on Beta male types to flatter them, entertain them, listen to them whine and complain about the frustrating behavior of Alpha males, and even spend money on them when they needed some financial assistance or support.

Instead, in today's society, Beta male types are either flat-out ignoring women, or they are treating 99% of the women they meet as if they are more of the kinky, promiscuous 'slut' types that are only worthy of providing them with an enjoyable and satisfying time in bed. Consequently, the vast majority of Beta male types are simply no longer interested in meeting a so-called 'good woman,' dating her for two or three years, proposing to her, and then marrying her and raising a family with her.

Where do we go from here? What can we expect in future?

I will discuss my answers to all of these questions in Part Three of this paperback.

Continue reading my friend.

PART THREE:

Dating for 21st Century Singles

In **Part Three**, I am going to offer a few of my 'harsh realities' of today's dating scene.

<u>Part Three is divided into eight chapters:</u>

Chapter Eight
The Diminishing Appeal of Strictly Monogamous Marriages: Where Do We Go from Here?

Chapter Nine
Examining the Men's Rights Movement (MRM) and Men Going Their Own Way (MGTOW)

Chapter Ten
Reality #1 of Today's Dating Scene: Alternative Relationships Have Diminished the Appeal of Strictly Monogamous Marriages

Chapter Eleven
Reality #2 of Today's Dating Scene: Alpha Males Do Not Like Spending Time with Women in a Platonic Manner ... and Now, Neither Do Beta Males

Chapter Twelve
Reality #3 of Today's Dating Scene: Men Have No Desire to 'Court' or 'Woo' a Woman Who They Have No Desire to Marry

Chapter Thirteen
Reality #4 of Today's Dating Scene: Many Beta Males are Dreadfully Afraid of What is Referred to as the 'Marital Bait-and-Switch' Routine

Chapter Fourteen
Reality #5 of Today's Dating Scene: Men Who Have Never Been Married and Do Not Have Any Children Can Afford to be 'Nitpicky' When Choosing a Wife

Chapter Fifteen
Reality #6 of Today's Dating Scene: Many Beta Male Types Who Previously Adored, Defended, and Worshipped Women Now HATE Them

I will then offer a brief 'Author's Wrap Up & Final Thoughts' at the very end.

Continue reading my friend.

Chapter Eight

The Diminishing Appeal of Strictly Monogamous Marriages: Where Do We Go from Here?

If you take time to read a number of blogs and dating-related internet message boards and discussion forums, and you also take time to listen to a number of talk radio programs and podcast programs that center on dating and relationships, you will inevitably find a number of (heterosexual) women blaming men for 90-99% of the problems in today's dating scene, and similarly, you will find a number of (heterosexual) men blaming women for 90-99% of the problems in today's dating scene.

The reality is, members of both genders are guilty of the problems in today's dating scene. Anyone who feels like the problems of today's dating scene are the fault of men only or women only is incredibly narrow-minded and delusional.

A lot of 'dating experts' attempt to make the problems in today's dating scene seem more 'complicated' than they are. In my mind, most of the problems in today's dating scene are very, very simple.

Alan Roger Currie

In a nutshell, there are just way too many men and women who are not upfront, specific, and straightforwardly honest with members of the opposite sex about **the exact type of romantic and sexual companionship that they really want**.

First, the misleading and manipulative ways of men:

You have men who will mislead women into believing that they are interested in a long-term sexual relationship, but in reality, these men really want a short-term sexual relationship.

You have men who will mislead women into believing that they are interested in a strictly monogamous sexual relationship or marriage, but in reality, these men really want to engage in promiscuous and/or polyamorous sex with multiple women.

You have men who will mislead women into believing that they are content with being a woman's 'play brother' or 'male girlfriend,' but in reality, these men want to be involved with these women in a romantic or sexual manner.

Next, the misleading and manipulative ways of women:

You have women who mislead men into believing that they never have, and never will engage in promiscuous and/or polyamorous sex, when the reality is, probably 4 out of every 5 women in society has engaged in at least a few episodes of short-term and/or non-monogamous 'casual' sex with SOME MAN.

You have women who mislead men into believing that they want to be that man's long-term girlfriend and/or future wife because they really, truly 'love' them ... when the reality is, these women really want to connect with a man simply because they know they can have their way this man (i.e., control the relationship and 'wear the pants') and they know they will be able to monopolize that man's financial resources in order to improve their overall quality of life.

You have women who will allow themselves to get pregnant by a man who has never once expressed an interest in marrying them and never once expressed an interest in raising children with them, and then when those men refuse to date them, marry them, and raise a family with them, they turn around and suggest that this man 'dogged them' and is an 'irresponsible parent.'

The main problem, as I see it, is that not too many men and women seem to be interested in engaging in romantic or sexual relationships that are mutually rewarding and beneficial, and full of honesty, sincerity, and genuine love and desire.

In the world of sports, the participants are very competitive because, at the end of the athletic event, they want to be labeled 'the winner.' In the world of athletic competition, that is how things are supposed to be. On the contrary, the world of dating and relationships is not supposed to be about one romantic companion 'winning' while the other sex partner 'loses.'

In the last couple of decades, many men have been guilty of leading women on and toying with their emotions, while many women have been guilty of leading men on and toying with their egos and their strong desire for sex. Both men and women deserve to be called out for behavior that is dishonest toward members of the opposite sex, that is disingenuous and duplicitous toward members of the opposite sex, and members of both genders need to be harshly admonished each time they are guilty of exhibiting blatantly misleading behavior and/or engaging in manipulative 'head games' with one another.

Members of both genders are guilty of lying to their spouses or long-term romantic companions and cheating on them with additional lovers behind their back. **This is wrong**.

The appeal of marriage, and more specifically, strictly monogamous marriages, has diminished greatly since 1970.

Look at the divorce rate in this country. It's ridiculously high.

The number of marriage proposals received by women who are 30 years of age or older has slowed to a crawl.

The reality of women is simply this: **NO WOMAN 'NEEDS' TO BE INVOLVED IN A LONG-TERM RELATIONSHIP or MARRIAGE TO SECURE A MAN'S SEXUAL COMPANIONSHIP. PERIOD.**

Every man needs to absorb this and fully understand this. Sexual attention and sexual companionship is NEVER a woman's **number one priority** for entering into a marriage or long-term romantic relationship. EVER. Any woman who possesses a reasonably attractive face and a reasonably sexy figure will always be able to gain a man's sexual attention and companionship if she really wants it.

Women's primary motivation for entering into a long-term romantic relationship is so a man can provide them with **a)** emotional empathy and support, **b)** financial assistance and support *(particularly if she is raising one or more children with her spouse or companion)*, and/or **c)** dependable non-sexual companionship and entertaining conversation. Regular or semi-regular sex is never higher than #2 in importance on her list of relationship priorities, and many times, it is not even on a woman's Top 5 list of her most important priorities;

Many times, women know when a man proposes to them that they are not really attracted to that man, but they go ahead and marry the guy because either **a)** he earns a lot of money and has offered to take care of her financially, **b)** her parents pretty much 'pressured her' to get married by a certain age, and/or **c)** they are 36 years of age or older and do not want to spend the rest of their life by themselves without any male companionship.

So, bottom line, men are not totally upfront and straightforwardly honest with the women they meet about their promiscuous and/or polyamorous ways because they feel that might cause them to 'miss out' on the opportunity to have sex with a woman who has made it clear to them that she is only willing to engage in sexual activities with men within the context of a strictly monogamous relationship or marriage.

Similarly, women fail to be totally upfront and straightforwardly honest with men about their promiscuous and/or polyamorous ways because women feel that the vast majority of men will deny them emotional support and access to their non-sexual companionship and/or financial resources.

Again, this is why most women hate the labels 'slut,' 'whore' and 'easy lay.' Even though all women are flattered by the fact that men find them physically attractive and sexually desirable, many women do not like it when they feel that a man only wants to spend time with them for the sole and specific purpose of exchanging orgasms and nothing else beyond that.

The only exception for most women would be men who they perceive to be *Total Alpha male* types. Women who have promiscuous and/or polyamorous tendencies don't mind engaging in strictly sexual relationships with *Total Alpha male* types. What they will do is usually find a *Total Beta male* type to provide them with flattering and entertaining non-sexual companionship when they desire it. And often, they will find themselves a wealthy, unmarried *Beta male with a few Alpha traits and tendencies* to fulfill the role of 'Sugar Daddy' for them.

Since I have already given my female readers the gist of what just about all men's dating advice centers on ('direct' vs. 'indirect' / PUA behavior), I will share with my male readers the gist of just about every dating advice book that is geared toward women that I have ever read or browsed through:

1) If you are genuinely a prudish and monogamy-oriented 'good girl', **STAY THAT WAY** by simply avoiding romantic and sexual interactions with any and all kinky and promiscuous *Total Alpha male* types! Once a 'good girl' gets 'turned out' by an erotically dominant Alpha male, 99% chance, there is no going back!! (i.e., that former 'good girl' will become addicted to the sexual companionship of Alpha males)

2) If you are more of a kinky and promiscuous and/or polyamorous type woman, do not allow any form of 'slut-shaming' to provoke you to change who you are and what you are about!! It is totally okay for women to 'sow their wild oats' with interested men in the same way that men have 'sowed their wild oats' with interested women for centuries!! Do not allow the infamous 'double-standard' to continue!

3)   If you are or used to be a kinky and promiscuous type woman ... but now, you want to 'transition' into being a more 'good girl' type in order to attract sexually conservative Beta males who are highly educated and earn a six or seven figure salary, **DO NOT SHARE ANY DETAILS ABOUT YOUR SEXUAL PAST** and your hot, kinky, satisfying sexual experiences with Alpha males!! Then, those wealthy Beta males will LOSE INTEREST!! Become a *Wholesome Pretender* and an *Erotic Hypocrite* when in the company of certified Beta males with high earning potential! (or for more short-term financial favors without actually going as far as to have sex with the Beta male, become a *Manipulative Timewaster* type)

4)   *(this one is the rarest of books for women, but ...)* **Enjoy the best of both worlds!!** Get yourself a hot, kinky, dominant 'Bull' and an obedient, financially generous 'Cuckold' and 'Sugar Daddy'!! Have them both serve your sexual needs, your non-sexual needs, and your financial needs at the same time without lying to any of them!!

As I lightheartedly expressed in Part Two of this paperback, the reason I can earn a living as a men's dating coach is because of **#3** above (I teach men - both Alpha males and Beta males - how to quickly and effectively identify *Wholesome Pretender* & *Erotic Hypocrite* types and *Manipulative Timewaster* types), and the main reason I can earn a living as a BDSM & Polyamory lifestyle Advisor and Consultant for women and couples is because of **#2** and **#4** above. I do not work with women for **#1** above. That is a hard lesson they are either going to have learn on their own or hope that their mother, father, big sister or big brother warns them.

So . . . what exactly needs to be modified in our dating rituals between men and women to create marriages and long-term romantic relationships that will be full of more honesty and sincerity and includes far less duplicity and manipulative 'head games?' What are some of the 'harsh realities' that each and every heterosexual single needs to be prepared for in today's dating scene?

I have some ideas that I will throw out to you in the upcoming chapters, but first, I am going to offer a quick review of the Men's Right's Movement and the MGTOW movement.

Continue reading my friend.

Chapter Nine

Examining the Men's Rights Movement (MRM) and Men Going Their Own Way (MGTOW)

A lot of men and women in society may not be aware, but there has been a percentage of men who have had a negative reaction to The Feminist Movement **for decades**.

The Men's Rights Movement started in the 1970s as 'The Men's Liberation Movement.' Here is an excerpt from Wikipedia:

The Men's Liberation Movement developed in the early 1970s among heterosexual, middle-class men in Britain and North America as a response to the cultural changes of the 1960s and 1970s, including the growth of the feminist movement, counterculture, women's and gay liberation movements, and the sexual revolution.

This movement later transitioned into being known as The Men's Rights Movement (MRM). MRM is different than what is known as 'Men Going Their Own Way' (or MGTOW). The latter is directly related to heterosexual men's current attitudes toward dating, relationships, sex, and marriage. MRM, on the other hand, has more to do with how men feel like the U.S.

Government's legal and judicial system seems to have an unfair bias toward protecting and benefiting the needs, preferences, and priorities of women ... and the thing is, even many women agree.

THE MEN'S RIGHTS MOVEMENT (MRM)

There are many (heterosexual) men in this country who feel like men are treated very unfairly when it comes to issues such as abortion, divorce, alimony payments, child support payments, child custody battles, domestic violence issues, false rape accusations, paternity fraud, financial assistance for men while being unemployed, as well as a number of other relevant issues for men in society.

Many men feel like there is an inherent 'bias' toward women in society, and that society treats men as if they are totally disposable compared to the lives and concerns of women.

The 2014 film, *Gone Girl*, addresses this issue in a subtle manner when you examine the conversations that take place between the characters of Nick Dunne (Actor Ben Affleck) and Attorney Tanner Bolt (Actor Tyler Perry).

Dunne is a cheating husband who has been set up and framed by his wife to make it look like he murdered her. When Dunne initially wants to blast his wife in the media, it is the smooth, savvy Bolt who informs Nick that he cannot just 'blatantly attack' women in the media. Bolt makes Dunne understand that bashing women in the media will only lead to public backlash because Bolt asserts that the general public always tends to side with women and generally offers women 'the benefit of the doubt' in a man vs. woman controversy.

Women have always been portrayed in the media and in movies and televisions programs as 'innocent victims' who are always being taken advantage of by 'mean-spirited, bullying men.' The reality is that invalid generalization is simply not true. There are good men in society, and there are no-good men in society. Similarly, there are good women in society, and there are no-good women in society. The percentage of 'good' and 'bad' members within each gender is realistically about equal.

Many divorce cases in society have frequently gone in favor of women regarding awarding women huge sums of money. This makes a lot of men very, very angry and leaves them feeling bitter toward women. Same with a lot of child support and child custody cases. I've known men personally who have told me that their ex-wives and/or women who were the mothers of their children have frequently denied them access to having regular interactions with their son(s) and/or daughter(s) even when the courts awarded them so many hours and days of custody per month.

It is hard for me to comment on many of these issues from personal experience, because I have never been married (at least, not as of the publishing of this paperback), and I currently do not have any children. I only hear stories from men I know personally, as well as the stories from disgruntled men that I have read about on blog sites, internet message boards and discussion forums, and other MANosphere-related materials.

For years, whenever a politician is running for public office, they always promise to 'look after the concerns of women.' Should they not be looking after the concerns of BOTH men and women? These media savvy politicians know exactly what they are doing.

I do not like any faction of society that attempts to demonize all men, and cause all men to be viewed as the 'bad guys' when it comes to male-female interactions and relationships. Are there men who are physically, verbally, and emotionally abusive to women? Yes. There is no doubt that evil men like this exist.

The reality is, there are also women in society who are more than capable of being physically, verbally, and emotionally abusive with their male spouses and romantic companions as well. The media does not seem to cover these incidents as much as they do with women. There are many evil women in society who don't like men at all.

These women are known as '**misandrists**.' A misandrist is a hater of men in the same way a **misogynist** is a hater of women. You don't hear the term 'misandrist' used in the media nearly as much as you hear the term 'misogynist' being used, and I believe this is very unfortunate. It is not fair to men at all.

I am all for men joining to identify objectively each and every one of the unfair practices that are currently in place in the U.S. legal and judicial system regarding a wide assortment of men's rights related issues. In that regard, I am all for MRM.

The only thing I would warn against is doing the same thing to women that many women do to men. Do not categorize ALL WOMEN as 'the bad guys.' There are a lot of women in society with good hearts and good intentions, and not all women are looking to take advantage of men in today's judicial system.

MEN GOING THEIR OWN WAY (MGTOW)

MGTOW members are more or less a 'sub-faction' of men who subscribe to the MANosphere in general. MGTOW members' main belief is that proposing marriage to women and entering into long-term monogamous type relationships with women is a total waste of time for men, and is even detrimental to their mental, emotional, and financial health in the long-run.

There is a small percentage of MGTOW members, despite being heterosexual, who believe in avoiding all social contact with women completely and indefinitely. They do not believe in flirting with women, asking women on dates, or even attempting to seduce women into engaging in casual sexual activities with them. They believe that men should simply concentrate on their own career-related and financial-related goals and objectives, and just forget about women completely. Essentially, they believe in becoming 'voluntarily asexual' or relying on indefinite episodes of masturbation for orgasmic pleasure.

The larger percentage of MGTOW members will still socially interact with women in small doses, and these men might even engage occasionally in a few episodes of short-term non-monogamous 'casual' sex with women, but they heavily frown on the idea of marriage, the idea of entering into a long-term monogamous 'boyfriend-girlfriend' type relationship, and the idea of 'wining and dining' women and spending money on women as any sort of 'Sugar Daddy' type in order to motivate women to have sex with them.

A lot of the men who read my eBooks and paperbacks, and listen to my audiobooks, are self-proclaimed 'MGTOW followers.' These men very much still want to engage in casual sex activities with women, but they have absolutely no desire to get engaged, get married, or have children with women. They believe that strictly monogamous marriages simply have no long-term benefits for men whatsoever. They also do not believe in being 'just friends' with women either. They have no desire to become a woman's 'play brother,' 'male girlfriend,' 'White Knight' or 'Captain Save-a-Ho.'

Raw truth? The vast majority of men who are *Total Alpha male* types have always been 'MGTOW' when it comes to spending time with women in a non-sexual manner. *Total Alpha male* types are all about one thing and one thing only: having sex with women and ejaculating their semen into women's mouths and vaginas. That's it. That is their number one motivation for socially interacting with women. They don't care about 'Lovey Dovey' romance stuff or playing the role of the 'boyfriend' or 'husband' to any woman. Most *Total Alpha male* types do not even want to assist a woman in raising children. If they were to have one or more sons, they would prefer to raise those sons themselves ... without any assistance from the woman who gave birth to them. Otherwise, they do not want anything to do with children.

What I am now going to do in the next six chapters of this paperback is offer six (6) very specific "harsh realities" regarding the idea of strictly monogamous marriages and other general thoughts about men and women's dating rituals in today's dating scene.

Many women will probably vehemently disagree with some of my strong opinions, and that is their right and prerogative to do so. I expect many philosophical disagreements. Even some men reading this paperback may find themselves having a philosophical disagreement with at least one or two of my strong assertions. If that ends up being the case, so be it.

The bottom line is, if society keeps pretending that nothing is wrong with dating and relationships between heterosexual men and heterosexual (and bisexual) women in today's society, then the degree of animosity between men and women is only going to continue to get worse. Fifty years from now, many heterosexual men will be engaging in sex with robots – that's right, female-like robots – instead of women (they have already been experimenting with these 'fembots' in Japan).

Continue reading my friend.

Chapter Ten

Reality #1 of Today's Dating Scene: Alternative Relationships Have Diminished the Appeal of Strictly Monogamous Marriages

If you have already read the first three chapters included in Part One of this paperback, you should now realize that initially, the idea of getting married had very little if anything to do with a man and woman's sexual attraction to each other or their feelings of 'true love' between one another. Those factors were conveniently added on later.

Hollywood and businesses looking to earn a profit were the primary entities in society that began placing extra emphasis on connecting the idea of 'being in love' with the goal of a man and a woman getting married. The reality is marriage, **from a legal standpoint**, should have nothing to do with one's emotional feelings and sexual attraction. Both of those factors are too fickle, impulsive, and unpredictable.

The entire notion of a strictly monogamous marriage is a man-made social construct. In other words, are you born with a 'natural' desire to get married one day? **No, you are not**.

Organized religion, books, movies, television, magazines, music videos, newspapers, and other societal influences brainwash you to believe in the notion of 'true love' and marriage.

A man or woman could feel like he or she is 'in love' with their spouse one day, and then later, after one or two episodes of adultery have been committed by their spouse, 90% or more of those 'loving feelings' have suddenly evaporated. A man or woman could have the strongest sense of 'sexual lust' for their husband or wife one month, but twenty-four to thirty-six months later, because their spouse is now ninety pounds heavier, their sense of insatiable sexual desire has now diminished almost entirely.

You can deny this fact all you want to, but no one can be guaranteed that 'true love' will last forever. You can HOPE and WISH that those feelings will last, but the realistic fact of the matter is, emotional feelings toward other human beings are just way too fluctuating, temperamental, and unstable. No man or woman should ever use their respective emotions as the foundation for what is supposed to be a permanent marital union.

The first harsh reality of today's dating scene I am going to express is this: the overall appeal of entering into a strictly monogamous marriage (for both men and women alike) has diminished greatly. There are just way too many 'alternative relationships' that are available to men and women that are mutually beneficial and rewarding that do not involve attempting to remain faithfully monogamous to one spouse until the day each one passes away.

Here are what I would rank as the Top 5 best alternatives to a strictly monogamous, traditional marriage in today's society:

- Sugar Daddy-Sugar Baby (or 'Sugar Mama-Stud') arrangements
- Bull-Cuckold-Hotwife arrangements
- Openly Polyamorous Marriages or Cohabitation relationships and Concubinage arrangements
- BDSM Erotic Domination & Submission relationships
- Purely Platonic Married or Unmarried 'Co-Parenting' Unions

There are many other types of alternative relationships, but for this paperback, I will primarily concentrate on these five very popular alternatives to the 19th Century and 20th Century 'old school' idea of strictly monogamous marriages.

SUGAR DADDY-SUGAR BABY
(or SUGAR MAMA-STUD) ARRANGEMENTS

Very few men I know who are 40 years of age or older who earn approximately $150,000 (USD) or more per year and have never been married and do not have any children have an interest in dating or marrying women who are near their age or older. A few exceptions? Sure. There are always exceptions.

Generally speaking, most men who are 40 years of age or older who are earning a six or seven-figure income are interested in dating women and engaging in sexual activities with women who are as young as 18 years of age and no older than roughly 35.

Arguably the top arrangement between an older man and a younger woman that comes the closest to being considered 'legalized prostitution' is what is known as a 'Sugar Daddy-Sugar Baby' relationship. (some alternative nicknames for 'Sugar Daddy' would be 'Sponsor,' 'Financial Provider,' and 'A Mature & Financially Generous Gentleman,' among other nicknames)

Why is this relationship legal, but prostitution illegal? Prostitution, in concept, centers around a direct exchange of money for sexual pleasure. For example, if I approach a woman, and I say, "I will give you fifty dollars if you agree to perform oral sex on me," that would be considered soliciting a woman for sexual services (i.e., prostitution), and that is illegal in all states except in many cities and counties in the state of Nevada.

When a man becomes a woman's 'Sugar Daddy,' he never offers to give the woman money directly in exchange for her providing him with sexual enjoyment and satisfaction. The woman who acts as the 'Sugar Baby' actually provides the man with her sexual companionship for **free** at her choice and discretion. What the man is actually spending money on is a woman's **non-sexual companionship** (which is legal), even though the man involved knows deep-down that he wants access to a combination of both the woman's sexual **and** non-sexual companionship.

The other characteristic of a Sugar Daddy-Sugar Baby relationship is that neither the man or the woman is obligated to offer each other anything for any set length of time. So, the man is not obligated to provide the woman with any financial favors or materialistic gifts for any specific length of time if he feels that the relationship is no longer beneficial to him. The Sugar Daddy can cut the relationship off at any time, just like the Sugar Baby is also free to cut the relationship off at any time she pleases.

Some men and women involved in these type of relationships have a 'verbal contract' between them, and others create a mutually agreed upon written contract that may specify the 'allowance' that the woman will be given, and the desired length of time that they both want the relationship to last.

The best thing to prevent blurring the line into the area of prostitution is for the Sugar Daddy to never, ever give the woman money directly before sex or directly after sex. Doing this can potentially place both the Sugar Daddy and the Sugar Baby in a compromising position that would bring unwanted legalities into play.

One method is for the man to hire the Sugar Baby candidate as a 'personal assistant,' but making sure to hire the woman as an 'independent contractor' instead of an employee who is a direct subordinate.

When a man hires a woman as a direct employee or subordinate, then she would be in a position to charge the man with sexual harassment if he hits on her for sex and she is not in the mood to reciprocate his sexual desires and interests.

When a man hires a woman as an 'independent contractor,' the woman is no longer in a position to charge the man with 'sexual harassment' or 'professional misconduct.' The only thing she can do is end her business collaboration with this particular man, and go about her way.

Another way that a man can pay a Sugar Baby 'indirectly' is to pay for many of her monthly or yearly expenses instead of paying her any money directly. This is what many Sugar Daddy types do. For example, the men will pay a woman's college tuition and room & board expenses for her, her medical bills, most of her utility bills, her rent or mortgage, and/or her automobile insurance payments and monthly car note.

The advantage of being a woman's Sugar Daddy is that as a man, you know this woman is essentially 'using you' for your financial resources and she knows that you are essentially 'using her' for her youth, her beauty, and her sexual companionship. You know this going into the relationship, so there are no real 'head games' going on.

Therefore, there is no way that a woman can get away with initially 'pretending' that she is 'truly in love with you,' but then unexpectedly blindsiding you by filing for divorce and trying to claim ownership to half of your financial and material assets and a good chunk of your personal property. In other words, the vast majority of older heterosexual men I know with means would much rather interact with a Sugar Baby type than a highly materialistic gold digger type masquerading as a fiancée or wife who is genuinely 'in love' with him when in reality she is simply plotting to take ownership of half of his financial assets and material possessions during divorce proceedings.

When a man goes as far as to marry a woman, he many times becomes obligated to provide that woman with a high-quality lifestyle even after he and the woman have divorced or are no longer attracted to each other. No man likes that.

On the other hand, with a Sugar Daddy-Sugar Baby arrangement, you are never obligated to provide a woman with a quality lifestyle for a length of time that you are not comfortable with. When you offer to be a woman's Sugar Daddy, you could limit your relationship with a woman to a few weeks, a few months, or maybe as long as four or five years. Some women have multiple Sugar Daddies, and some men have multiple Sugar Babies. There are even websites available in today's society that offer to match a Sugar Daddy candidate with a Sugar Baby candidate. And again ... this is all **totally legal**.

Generally speaking, the status of 'Sugar Baby' is usually reserved for women between the ages of 18 and 29, or maybe 18 and 35. A woman who is between 36 and 39 would be on the borderline for most Sugar Daddy types. As with anything, there are always exceptions. I once met a woman who was 45 years old who was a Sugar Baby for a man who was 68 years old.

An older companion providing a younger companion with financial favors is not limited to only older men and younger women. The similar arrangement on the female side is commonly known as either a 'Sugar Mama-Stud' relationship or a 'Cougar-Cub' relationship. The latter does not usually involve financial favors, but sometimes it does.

There are some women in society who are 40 years of age or older and earn a six or seven figure salary who will offer men as young as 18 and as old as 35 a certain degree of 'financial favors' in exchange for their sexual and non-sexual companionship. Especially if the man is a *Total Alpha male* type.

In the mid-1990s, while residing in Los Angeles, I engaged in a couple of short-term 'Sugar Mama-Stud' relationships. One lasted for a little over a year, and another lasted for about six or seven months. There are a lot of women in society who are between 36 and 59 who have money who get very lonely and horny for male companionship to the point where they are willing to financially compensate a man – and particularly a man who is 35 years of age or younger – for both his sexual and non-sexual companionship.

Again, the advantage that these type of 'arrangements' have over marriage is that neither the man or woman involved feels 'obligated' to keep the relationship going once it has fully run its course. Once the attraction and chemistry begin to diminish, the two people involved simply mutually agree to end the relationship and move on with their lives.

If you are a man or woman who does not consider yourself 'shallow' or 'superficial,' then I would not recommend Sugar dating to you. On the other hand, if you are realistic with yourself, and you know deep-down that you just want to exchange financial favors for youth, beauty, and sex appeal, then Sugar dating is the answer.

Given a choice, I would much rather be exploited for my financial resources as a 'Sugar Daddy' than to be a *Beta male with a few Alpha traits and tendencies* type in a disingenuous marriage, and be 'used' for my financial resources and material assets by a materialistic and manipulative woman who never loved me to begin with … and to add insult to injury, that materialistic wife can potentially gain access to as much as half of your net worth in a divorce. Stick with the 'Sugar Baby.'

If you are a man earning less than six figures, I would not even think about becoming a Sugar Daddy. It will be a waste of your time and most women's time.

BULL-CUCKOLD-HOTWIFE ARRANGEMENTS

There are some in the media who have proclaimed what is known as a 'Bull-Cuckold-Hotwife' arrangement as the top 'alternative relationship' that is growing the fastest in popularity in today's society.

This relationship, or 'arrangement,' tends to blend elements of the BDSM (Erotic Domination & Erotic Submission) lifestyle with elements of the Polyamory lifestyle.

In the world of BDSM, there are primarily four types of sexual personalities:

- Top / Dom / Master / Mistress
- Switch
- Flexible or Versatile
- Bottom / Sub / Slave

A 'Top / Dom / Master / Mistress' is a man or woman who enjoys being the erotically dominant partner no less than 99% of the time, and is the sex partner who issues out the commands and requests to their erotically submissive partner(s);

A 'Bottom / Sub / Slave' is a man or woman who enjoys being the erotically submissive partner no less than 99% of the time, and is the sex partner who always seeks to be obedient to the commands and requests of their erotically dominant partner(s);

A 'Switch' is a man or woman who is erotically dominant with at least one sex partner, but they are also completely erotically submissive with at least one totally different sex partner;

A 'Flexible' or 'Versatile' is a man or woman who vacillates between being an erotically dominant partner and an erotically submissive partner with the same spouse or the same exact romantic or sexual companion.

In a 'Bull-Cuckold-Hotwife' arrangement, the 'Bull' would be a man who has the personality and demeanor of a *Total Alpha male* type. The Bull would be the 'Top' or 'Dom' in the relationship. The Bull many times dominates both the Hotwife and the Cuckold, or in some cases, he just dominates the Hotwife, and he allows the Hotwife to dominate the Cuckold exclusively.

The woman involved – regardless of whether she is married, engaged, or unmarried – is referred to as the 'Hotwife.' She is the 'Switch' in the relationship. The Hotwife is totally erotically submissive to her Bull (or Bulls ... many times, she has more than one), but she is totally erotically dominant with her Cuckold. She usually allows her Cuckold to play the role of 'obedient and submissive voyeur' who watches her engage in sexual activities with her Bull(s) while he masturbates and then he usually cleans both the Bull's penis and the Hotwife's vagina when their episode of orgasmic pleasure has concluded.

The Cuckold would be a man who has the personality and demeanor of either a *Total Beta male* type or in some cases, a *Beta male with a few Alpha traits and tendencies.* The Cuckold would be the 'Sub,' 'Bottom,' or 'Slave' in this arrangement. The Cuckold's job is to obey everything the Hotwife tells him to do and to prepare her body to have sex with her designated Bulls.

Most of the time, the Cuckold only rarely gains the opportunity to engage in vaginal intercourse with the Hotwife. The vast majority of the time, the Cuckold only gains the opportunity to perform oral sex on his Hotwife before the Bull engages in sexual activities with the Hotwife. Many times, he also has to perform oral sex on the Hotwife after the Bull has ejaculated into the Hotwife's vagina.

This arrangement is sort of like combining the aforementioned 'Sugar Mama-Stud' relationship with a 'Sugar Daddy-Sugar Baby' relationship, with the only difference being that the 'Stud' involved is a very erotically dominant 'Bull' and the 'Sugar Daddy' involved is a very obedient and erotically submissive 'Cuckold.'

Most Bulls usually possess a very athletic physique and an above-average sized penis. Sometimes, the Bull is identified by his race if the other two partners are of a different ethnicity. For example, if the Bull is African-American, and the Hotwife and Cuckold are both Caucasian, then he would be referred to as a 'Black Bull.' If the Bull is a Latino or Spaniard, he will be referred to as a 'Latin Bull.' The key personality characteristic for a Bull type is that he absolutely has to be a combination of very kinky and extremely erotically dominant with women.

Cuckold types are usually men who seek to share the company of a woman who is considered 'out of their league.' Many Cuckolds are as young as roughly 25 years old, and as old as in their sixties or seventies. Cuckolds usually earn no less than high five figures, and as much as seven figures. If the Cuckold is older, he usually has erectile dysfunction problems or sexual impotence and stamina problems. If the Cuckold is younger, he usually feels very 'egotistically insecure' regarding his ability to please and satisfy a woman in bed, and he typically possesses a less-than-average-sized penis.

The key personality trait for a Cuckold type is that he loves to be dominated by women, and even verbally disrespected and humiliated by women. Some say this comes from the man having a mother or step-mother who was extremely dominant with them and used to browbeat them as a child or teenager.

Hotwife types are women who want to 'have their cake and eat it too.' These are women who want to enjoy the seductive charm and sexual prowess offered by the typical *Total Alpha male* type, but they also want to take advantage of both the financial resources and the non-sexual companionship that a *Beta male with a few Alpha traits and tendencies* or a *Total Beta male* type has to offer them. They are usually very attractive and maintain a figure that is very athletically toned and her weight is very well proportioned.

In some cases, the Hotwife and the Cuckold will be legally married, but in many other cases, they will engage in a long-term version of a 'Sugar Daddy-Sugar Baby' arrangement. Obviously, if the two are married, it is not a strictly monogamous marriage between the two (many times, the Cuckold will remain faithfully and obediently monogamous to his Hotwife, while the Hotwife is free to see as many men as she chooses to). In a nutshell, the Cuckold is the Hotwife's 'bitch.'

I would recommend this type of arrangement for men who are *Total Beta male* types who have absolutely no desire to become more 'Alpha.' If you have no desire to make any changes or improvements mentally, physically, sexually, and otherwise, then being a woman's bitch is probably better than you sitting at home jerking off to Internet pornography. At least in this scenario, when you jerk off, you are jerking off to live sex taking place in front of your eyes.

OPENLY POLYAMOROUS MARRIAGES or COHABITATION RELATIONSHIPS and CONCUBINAGE ARRANGEMENTS

I mentioned in an earlier chapter that the marital arrangement that comes the closest to representing 'legal polygamy' is when a man is married, but he also has one or more concubines. A concubine is an additional lover or 'openly known mistress' for a married man that his wife knows about, approves of, and even socially interacts with regularly.

Many times, a married man's concubine will reside in the same household as the married couple, and might even take on household responsibilities such as functioning as the married couple's nanny, housekeeper, or cook and personal chef.

There are many men who live in cultures and cultures where concubinage is considered totally normal and acceptable, although here in the United States, many men and women are unfamiliar with this concept and may find it a bit 'strange.'

When a married man has one or more concubines, usually he and his wife establish a certain set of 'parameters' for the concubines. For example, usually, the concubine can never allow herself to get pregnant by the married man. Also, the wife always gets first preference over when she can have sex with her husband.

Concubinage is a very effective form of engaging in an openly polyamorous marriage in a situation where the wife only wants to engage in sexual activities with her husband, but she has no problems with her husband engaging in sexual activities with one or more additional lovers. Technically, a wife can also take on one or more male concubines herself, but that scenario is very rare. A Bull-Cuckold-Hotwife arrangement tends to replace a woman's need for male concubines.

Many unmarried couples who enjoy an openly polyamorous lifestyle simply tend to cohabitate instead of getting married. In some cases, they may cohabitate with multiple other openly polyamorous couples. This is known in the Polyamory lifestyle as a 'Polyamorous Family.'

For example, if three unmarried polyamorous couples pool their resources together and purchase a house for all six of them, and each of the three male companions is having sex with each of the three female companions, this would represent a Polyamorous Family. In other situations, you might have two or more unmarried polyamorous couples who reside in the same apartment or townhouse complex or the same subdivision.

There are some married couples who engage in an openly polyamorous union. The married couple will usually engage in sex with each other, and also, each will have other designated lovers that their spouse knows about and approves of. One form of polyamorous dating among married couples is known as 'couple-swapping.' There are many married couples who are openly polyamorous who regularly engage in sexual activities with other married couples.

These types of arrangements and relationships have become very popular among a lot of polyamorous men and women in the 21st Century. Polyamory is considered by most to be a 'middle-of-the-road' compromise between strict monogamy and wild, wide-open promiscuity. When you are openly polyamorous, you gain the opportunity to enjoy sex with two or more companions, but at the same time, your multiple sex partners are approved of by all of your other sex partners, and everyone makes sure that all of their chosen partners remain STD free.

Many men who are *Total Alpha male* types have engaged in openly polyamorous relationships and marriages for centuries. *Total Alpha male* types have never believed in strict monogamy (although they will usually welcome a woman who offers to be strictly monogamous to them).

There is an adage that goes, "if you truly love someone, give them the freedom to interact with others romantically and sexually. If after their experiences, they come back to you and only want to be with you, then that person was always yours. If you never hear from them again after their experiences with others, then that means they were never yours in the first place."

BDSM (Erotic Domination & Submission) RELATIONSHIPS

What if you took a Bull-Cuckold-Hotwife arrangement, and you eliminated either the 'Bull' or 'Cuckold' out of the relationship? In the world of the BDSM lifestyle, this would be known simply as an 'Erotically Dominant / Submissive' relationship. A BDSM relationship can be strictly monogamous or openly polyamorous.

Most long-term BDSM relationships are usually between an erotically dominant man and an erotically submissive woman.

Rarely will you find a high number of BDSM relationships that include an erotically dominant woman and an erotically submissive man, except the more popular Bull-Cuckold-Hotwife arrangement.

If the erotically submissive partner is strictly monogamous to her erotically dominant male partner, this means that she has been 'collared.' This means that this particular BDSM sub can only obey the commands and requests of her BDSM Dom. She can no longer take orders or satisfy requests for any other male dominant other than her one Master.

If a BDSM sub is not collared, then this means that she can have two or more BDSM Dominants in her life if she so chooses. Many male Doms share one or more of their submissives with other male Doms to enjoy sexually.

BDSM relationships are very appealing to men who do not like being romantically or sexually involved with women who they consider to be 'too bossy,' 'too moody,' 'too argumentative,' and 'too demanding' and 'high maintenance.'

Beginning with 2010, I have assisted many men and women in making the transition from a conventional, traditional, strictly monogamous relationship or marriage to one that has more BDSM and/or Polyamory undertones to them.

A study was released in 2013 that said that men and women who are involved in the BDSM lifestyle experienced 'better mental health' than those involved in conventional marriages or romantic relationships, and they experienced fewer arguments and disagreements as well as a higher degree of romantic and sexual passion than those involved in traditional relationships.

Based on my many experiences and observations, I would have to agree. My relationships with women that have been of a BDSM nature were MUCH more enjoyable and satisfying than my romantic or sexual relationships with women that did not include any erotic domination and submission themes.

Personally, I am not too heavy on the physical side of BDSM (e.g., flogging, handcuffing, whipping, tying up women with ropes, paddling, among other activities). The most physical form of BDSM that I have engaged in is hand-spanking the naked buttocks of a BDSM sub when she has been disobedient or smart-alecky with me. Verbally and psychologically, I am usually extremely erotically dominant with my BDSM subs.

Many BDSM companions sign written contracts so that they can agree upon what is allowed and what will not be allowed. Your BDSM subs are allowed to use at least two 'Safewords' whenever they feel uncomfortable with a sexual situation:

- 'Yellow' or 'Banana' means that your BDSM sub does not necessarily want you to stop what you are doing, but they do want you to slow down and reduce the level of physical force or verbal harshness you may be displaying with them;

- 'Red' or 'Strawberry' means that your BDSM sub wants you to stop whatever it is you are doing immediately because of either some physical pain or discomfort, some emotional pain or discomfort, or because a child, acquaintance, family member, or unknown visitor has entered the room or the residential premises unexpectedly.

Think of Safewords like a traffic light. A yellow traffic light means 'caution ... slow down' and a red traffic light means 'stop ... right now!' It's the same with BDSM Safewords.

Not everyone is cut out to participate in the BDSM lifestyle and/or Polyamory lifestyle. For example, if you are a man or woman who becomes very angry and jealous when you see your romantic companion or steady sex partner being flirtatious with other members of the opposite sex, then you should just stick to strictly monogamous romantic relationships and marriages.

I would recommend the BDSM lifestyle to any Beta male type who wants to 'reclaim' his sense of manhood and masculinity. Realistically, you are only going to go in one of two directions: Either your 'suppressed Alpha side' is going to be unleashed, or your true submissive Beta side is going to become more pronounced. Either, or. There you have it.

PURELY PLATONIC MARRIAGES and UNMARRIED CO-PARENTING UNIONS

Sometimes men and women in society tend to assume that if the parents of one or more children reside in the same household, that it automatically means the married or unmarried parents are 'deeply in love' and engaging in sexual activities on a regular or semi-regular basis. This is not necessarily true in today's more free-spirited dating climate.

A very underrated and overlooked arrangement that some parents of children engage in is what is known as a purely platonic 'co-parenting union.' The parents can be unmarried or married and openly polyamorous.

A man or woman's emotional feelings and sexual desires should have nothing to do with their desire to raise children in a healthy, drama-free environment. To take it a step further, sometimes a Gay man will impregnate (either via intercourse or through artificial insemination) a woman who is just a 'very good friend' of his, and the two will agree to raise the children together until their youngest child graduates from high school or college. Raising children with your 'best friend' who is a member of the opposite sex can be very rewarding for men and women.

Filmmaker Spike Lee's 2004 film, *She Hate Me*, centered around a similar situation involving a Lesbian Woman (Actress Kerry Washington) who desires to get pregnant and raise a child with one of her platonic male friends (Actor Anthony Mackie).

The clear advantage of these type of relationships (or 'arrangements') is that you do not allow the fickle, impulsive, and unpredictable nature of your emotional feelings toward someone or your constantly fluctuating desire to have sex with this person to interfere with your desire to have both biological parents raise one or more children without major problems or arguments.

This type of arrangement prevents contentious child support battles and child custody disagreements. The objective of the parents is simply to raise their children. This situation is ideal for men and women who know they possess a very promiscuous and/or polyamorous nature, but they still want to be in a situation to raise children without a lot of 'unnecessary drama' or constantly changing step-mothers and step-fathers being involved throughout the course of their children's life.

If there is one period in a woman's life when many of them will seek out this type of arrangement with a male friend who they trust is when they know their 'biological clock' is coming to an end, and they want to give birth to at least one child before they hit their menopause stage. Many times, if the woman is wealthy or financially self-sufficient, she will sign a contract legally waiving any child support payments from the biological father.

This option is a great option for women who are roughly 35 years of age or older who have never been married and never given birth to a child, but who very badly want to raise at least one child, and they want some degree of non-financial assistance and support from a man in doing so.

So, as you can surmise, there are a lot of alternative options men and women have in today's society other than to enter into a strictly monogamous marriage or strictly monogamous cohabitation situation. One service I would look into if you are considering experimenting with any form of openly polyamorous relationships is one called XOXY. Once you become a registered subscriber of XOXY.com, men and women will know that you **a)** have no (recent) history of testing positive for sexually transmitted diseases and **b)** you have no history of violent crimes and sexual-related felonies. I believe this service might help revolutionize openly polyamorous marriages and relationships in today's society.

In the next chapter, I will offer my very next '21st Century Dating Reality' which centers on the fact that just about all Alpha males hate spending too much time with women in a non-sexual manner, but because of The Beta Male Revolution, now ... most Beta males feel the exact same way.

Continue reading my friend.

Chapter Eleven

Reality #2 of Today's Dating Scene:
Alpha Males Do Not Like Spending Time with
Women in a Platonic Manner ...
and Now, Neither Do Beta Males

Lighthearted 'disclaimer': If you are an Alpha male type reading this paperback, you might as well skip this chapter. This chapter is representative of me 'preaching to the choir.' Also, if you read my other book entitled, *The Possibility of Sex: How Naïve and Lustful Men are Manipulated by Women Regularly*, then you already know where this chapter is going. This chapter is for the Beta male types and the women ... and particularly, women who are very naïve and delusional about men's real motivations to spend time with them.

If you are a woman reading this paperback, let me make something very, very clear to you:

Men, generally speaking, have no interest in maintaining a purely platonic 'friendship' with a woman who they find physically attractive and sexually appealing. Period.

I remember when I was young, I would often hear some women refer to a man who was in his forties, fifties, or sixties as a 'dirty old man' if he flirted with women in a sexually provocative manner, particularly if the women were younger than him.

Now that I am 53 years old, I am here to proclaim: There is **no such thing** as a 'dirty old man.' That term is a myth perpetuated by delusional women.

Speaking for myself and most men I know who are in my same age group, it is not that a man gets 'hornier for sex' as he gets older. I would make the argument that the vast majority of men's desire for sex usually *decreases* to one degree or another as they get older.

The reason it seems like men get hornier and more lustful as they get older is because their desire and tolerance for being around women in a non-physical, non-sexual, purely platonic manner **drops drastically**.

Pretend you are looking at a graph with two vertically rectangle graph bars side by side. One vertical rectangle represents my desire to spend time with women sexually, and the other vertical rectangle represents my desire to spend time with women non-sexually.

On a scale from 1-100, when I was 23 years old, my level of desire to spend time with women sexually was probably somewhere between 95 and 100, and my level of desire to spend time with women non-sexually was probably somewhere between 45 and 50. Now that I am 53, my level of desire to spend time with women sexually is probably between 75 and 80, and my level of desire to spend time with women non-sexually is probably between 5 and 10 ... and that is being very generous regarding the non-sexual rating.

Business and professional-related collaborations and interactions aside, I simply have very little if any desire or enthusiasm toward spending time with women in a purely platonic manner. A woman's non-sexual companionship does nothing for me. Nothing.

The thing is, I know for a fact that I am not alone. Just about every Alpha male type I know has shared with me the same sentiments. The only men I know, generally speaking, who have a high tolerance for being around women regularly in a purely platonic manner are usually Beta male types.

Alpha males either want to be around women strictly for sexual purposes or at minimum, a blend of sexual and non-sexual companionship. The worst is the men who I have categorized in this paperback as the *Total Alpha male* type. Men in this category absolutely hate spending a significant amount of time with women in a non-physical, non-sexual manner. They simply have no interest.

A man who is an *Alpha male with a few Beta traits and tendencies* will do a much better job of tolerating being around a woman he truly cares for and loves in a non-sexual manner, but even these men do not like to spend too much time with women in a non-physical, non-sexual manner when their primary objective is short-term and/or non-monogamous sex.

I believe that the vast majority of 'platonic friendships' between single heterosexual men and women are disingenuous. As mentioned in my other eBooks, paperbacks, and audiobooks, I refer to disingenuous friendships between men and women as **FunClubbing**.

Anytime you are 'pretending' to be content with being 'just friends' with a member of the opposite sex, but you know deep-down that you would rather be engaging in a series of social interactions with that person that include a high degree of romantic and/or sexual undertones to them, then this means that you are guilty of *FunClubbing* with that person.

One of the reasons why I hate watching most television shows as well as a lot of romantic comedies and dramas is because they always show men being totally enthusiastic about being a good looking, sexy woman's 'male girlfriend' or 'play brother.' That is so unrealistic.

Real talk: Women love being around men in a purely platonic manner **much more** than the average man loves being around women in a purely platonic manner.

Most men – and particularly Alpha males – are either content being by themselves, or they prefer the company of other men in situations when they are not feeling particularly horny.

One story I have told to my talk radio listeners probably two dozen times was about when I was a part of this very regimented, borderline 'cult-like' church in Los Angeles between late Summer of 1994 and December of 1996.

Arguably the single most interesting sermon I ever listened to attentively was when this guest minister was preaching about how men and women should avoid premarital sex, and they should ideally wait until marriage to engage in sexual activities with each other.

More specifically within that same sermon, he expressed his harsh criticisms regarding what he felt was a significant increase in the number of 'purely platonic friendships' between single men and single women in today's society.

He said (paraphrasing a bit), "I am not a fan of single men and single women maintaining all of these platonic friendships with each other. This delays your goal of finding your husband or wife. There is no part of the Bible where God or Jesus Christ encourages men to maintain a high number of platonic friends with women. God did not place human beings with two different set of genitalia on Earth for them to nurture and maintain a platonic friendship with each other. No sir. God placed men and women on Earth to date, mate, and reproduce themselves. This is what you all need to be doing. Date, mate, and reproduce yourselves. That is your number one mission here on Earth."

I probably yelled out the loudest 'Amen' in response to his comments than I ever have in my personal history of attending a Sunday morning church service.

Speaking of my time spent in that church in Los Angeles, here was the interesting thing I noticed: very few of the men behaved in a sexually aggressive manner toward the women in the church. Just about all of the men in the church behaved like sexually self-controlled and respectful 'gentlemen' toward the women in the church. Matter of fact, there were more incidents of the women in the church being sexually aggressive with the men than vice versa. This was an epiphany for me.

What I have come to realize is this: Most men have a much harder time being around women in a purely platonic manner when they know those women are regularly engaging in sexual activities with other men outside the context of a husband-wife relationship or a long-term 'boyfriend-girlfriend' relationship.

If you place the average man in a social situation where he knows that the women he is socializing with are very sexually active, and even more so, very promiscuous, his sexually aggressive tendencies are going to begin to reveal themselves. This is what I feel contributes highly to men committing date-rape with women and sexual assault with women.

Do your research. There were not too many cases of rape and date-rape on college campuses before the Sexual Revolution took place in the 1960s and early 1970s. Most men in the early to middle portion of the 20th Century would be dreadfully afraid of attempting to date-rape or sexually assault a woman, because most women's fathers were extremely overprotective, if not flat-out crazy (I joke with people all the time, the fear of receiving retribution from a woman's psychotic father is the most effective deterrent to sexual aggression by a man).

In today's society, incidents of rape, date-rape, and sexual assault happens almost on a weekly basis. In my opinion, this is no accident. It is not so much that men's behavior has changed for the worse, but I would argue that more specifically, *men's perceptions and assumptions regarding women's sexual behavior* has dramatically changed in the last few decades.

In blunt terms, most men today tend to view most women in today's society as being very promiscuous. And this perception has caused men to become much more sexually aggressive with women when they feel they are in the company of a woman who is very sexually active and promiscuous (especially if the woman has alcohol in their system) than they do when they are in the company of a woman who they perceive to be a virgin, a woman practicing premarital celibacy, or a woman who they perceive to be extremely prudish and strictly monogamy-oriented.

Total Alpha male types are going to be the least likely to commit date-rape or attempt to sexually assault a woman (with the exception of instances where they may be inebriated). Total Alpha types are very egotistical, and consequently, they expect most women to 'throw themselves at them.' So, because of that, they rarely are inappropriately or excessively aggressive with women of interest.

Alpha male with a few Beta traits and tendencies types are not going to be too sexually aggressive with women (again, unless they happen to be inebriated at the time). Men in this category will seek to 'test' some women to see if they are a more of a prudish and monogamy-oriented 'good girl' type or more of a kinky and promiscuous and/or polyamorous type, but it is highly doubtful that they will go as far as to (knowingly or intentionally) date-rape or sexually assault a woman.

Beta male with a few Alpha traits and tendencies types can be very 'passive-aggressive' and emotionally volatile at times. Therefore, men in this category have an extremely hard time tolerating what they perceive to be 'mixed signals' from a woman of interest. For example, if a woman is flirtatious with a man in this category, but she may not be 100% enthusiastic about engaging in vaginal intercourse, a good number of men in this category may find themselves becoming 'inappropriately aggressive' with women because of their emotional and egotistical frustration. Advice to men in this category: **Be direct**. Make sure the women you are looking to engage in oral sex with, anal sex with, and vaginal intercourse with are 100% interested in allowing you to do so. Do not accept 'vague and ambiguous' responses. Advice to women: **Be very firm, specific, and definite regarding your 'yes' and 'no' responses**. Don't find yourself in a 'compromising position' when you know it could have been prevented and avoided.

Total Beta male types tend to include a lot of men who possess 'psychopath' or 'sociopath' type proclivities. Many men in this category have gone months, years, or even decades without sexual interaction with women. Sometimes, they reach a point where they simply cannot control their level of sexual desire and sexual frustration any longer. Some men in this category are like a 'time-bomb' of sexuality waiting to happen.

The hardcore truth is that very few men can handle the feeling of being 'left out of the fun' that other men are enjoying with women. For some men, particularly those who are mentally and emotionally unstable or men who have a boat load of testosterone in their system, this situation brings out a lot of men's 'dark side' and violent side.

There is a joke I have heard a number of times: "What is the difference between a 'ho' and a 'bitch'? A ho is a woman who is having sex with every man in your neighborhood INCLUDING you. A bitch is a woman who is having sex with every man in your neighborhood EXCEPT you."

I now speak to many men and women on college campuses about date-rape prevention and sexual assault prevention (in association with an organization entitled *Take Back The Night*). Both men and women need to be enlightened on what goes on in the minds of the opposite sex to prevent 'compromising situations.' **Upfront, specific, straight-to-the-point verbal communication is key**.

Many men I have met over the years actually do refer to women as 'bitches' when they feel like a woman is willing to have sex with every guy in their social circle BUT him.

No woman should seek to develop a long-lasting friendship with a man who she knows has some sort of romantic or sexual attraction to her. I would emphatically warn women against doing this. You are almost asking for that man to become sexually aggressive toward you at some point.

My recommendation is that a woman only seek to maintain purely platonic friendships with men who they are convinced have no desire to date them and have no desire to engage in casual sex with them.

How do you find out a man's true motivations? **Ask him if he is interested in having sex with you.** Ask this so-called 'platonic friend' of yours, "[insert man's first name here], if I offered you the opportunity to engage in sexual activities with me, would you be willing to have sex with me?" Preferably, you should ask the man this question in a relatively 'safe' environment (e.g., a public library, restaurant, bookstore, etc.).

If the man flat-out turns you down, then he is worth keeping as a platonic friend. If the man either quickly reciprocates your offer of sex or gives you a long, heartfelt speech ... but then later reciprocates your offer of sex ... then that man is not 'platonic friend' material. Note: **Do not ask a man this question while he has drugs or alcohol in his system.**

Most women are not going to take heed to any of my advice in this chapter simply because **the vast majority of women love male attention too much**. This goes back to why most women love the companionship of Beta males.

Beta males are far more likely than Alpha males to invest a significant amount of time flattering women, entertaining women, and 'wining and dining' women – particularly women who have yet to confirm an interest in having sex with them.

If a woman is not offering an Alpha male type either her sexual companionship or a blend of her sexual and non-sexual companionship, Alpha male types are not going to be interested in spending time with any woman more than maybe once or twice.

Women need to recognize the biological tendencies and true motivations of men. Do not allow yourselves to remain naïve and delusional. You may think playfully 'teasing' your platonic male friend in a sexual manner is 'fun' and egotistically satisfying, but I am warning you: you are playing with fire, and **one day you are going to get burned**. Trust.

NO HETEROSEXUAL MAN GENUINELY WANTS TO MAINTAIN A PURELY PLATONIC FRIENDSHIP WITH A WOMAN INDEFINITELY IF HE FINDS THAT WOMAN TO BE PHYSICALLY ATTRACTIVE and SEXUALLY APPEALING.

Don't be fooled by men who are doing an Academy Award winning job of *FunClubbing*. Those men are just waiting for the right time on the right day to make their move.

In the next chapter, I am going to discuss an issue that is similar to the subject matter of this chapter, and that is the fact that most Beta male types in today's society are no longer falling for the 'That Alpha male treated me so badly ... and now I need a nice, sweet Beta male to rescue me' sob story routine.

Most Beta males today no longer look at Alpha male types as the 'bad guys.' They more so look at sexually duplicitous, highly manipulative and materialistic women as the 'bad guys.'

Continue reading my friend.

Chapter Twelve

Reality #3 of Today's Dating Scene: Men Have No Desire to 'Court' or 'Woo' a Woman Who They Have No Desire to Marry

Women. Bless their little naïve and delusional hearts.

One of the most frequent complaints I receive from (single) women is, "Alan, why don't men seek to 'court' us and 'woo' us anymore? It seems as though every man I meet is just looking to jump right into the sack with me. I think that is so shallow!"

Don't blame men. Blame the other members of your gender. Think about it: If you always had to pay for the food at your favorite restaurant … but then, all of the sudden you saw other patrons of that restaurant receiving the same food you are eating for FREE … would you be motivated to continue paying for that food? No. You would not.

The Same concept applies to male-female relationships. Beta males no longer want to invest a significant amount time and money 'wining and dining' women who are not guaranteeing these men that they are willing to have sex with them when they see *Total Alpha male* types and *Alpha male with a few Beta traits and tendencies* types getting women in bed without spending any money on them and without promising them any long-term monogamy. To do so would be economic stupidity.

If you read my book, *Mode One: Let the Women Know What You're REALLY Thinking*, I discuss this scenario in Chapter Five. I remember once I was at a nightclub, and there was this guy who had spent a lot of time with this woman non-sexually, and he spent a lot of money on her ... and he had not even had sex with her yet. When this same guy mentioned the woman's name to these other two guys at the club, they started laughing.

Long story short, the two guys who were laughing ended up letting the naïve Beta male type know that they had both had sex with this woman within a few hours after meeting her, and they spent no money on her nor did they spend any time with her non-sexually. Soon, the Beta male guy was **seething** with anger.

You see, there was a time when many women who were sexually duplicitous and highly manipulative covert 'gold digger' types were able to get over on and seduce Beta male types into long-term relationships with ease. How would they do it?

Easy. They would paint the picture for Beta male types that all men who were womanizing Alpha male types were the 'wolves in sheep's clothing,' and that they were the 'innocent victims' who got 'used and abused' by these lying, selfish men.

Riiiiiiiiiiiiiiiiiiiiiiiiiiight.

Then came the knowledge, wisdom, and advice offered in the MANosphere, and everything changed. Beta male types began to slowly but surely realize, **these women knew what they were doing**. These men realized that the vast majority of women who have interacted with Alpha male types sexually did so **because they simply wanted to**. Not because they were 'tricked' into having sex or 'coerced' into having sex by 'mean, conniving, or forceful' Alpha males.

I repeat once again: Women who are kinky, women who are very feminine and submissive, and women who possess a high degree of promiscuous and/or polyamorous tendencies are **always** going to prefer the sexual companionship of an Alpha male type over the sexual companionship of a Beta male type. *These women would go crazy* if all Alpha male types were to decide suddenly that they wanted to be strictly monogamous with women. **These women would go nuts.**

I am going to let you men in on a little secret about women: The vast majority of women **get bored** when men always treat them as the 'good girl' type. They are flattered by that, and they find it representative of a man being a respectful 'gentleman' and all, but beyond that, it bores them to death.

When a woman's interest in you is financial assistance and support, and entertaining conversation and enjoyable non-sexual social companionship, then yes ... she wants to be treated like the 'respectable good girl.'

When a woman is horny, wants a man to bang her hard and cause her to experience multiple orgasms, the least thing she wants from a man is for that man to treat her like a 'good girl' type. She wants to be treated like a kinky slut in the bedroom. Even this somewhat pretentious and prudish female guest I interviewed once on my talk radio show admitted that. She said, *"I will agree Alan ... **every woman wants to be treated like a slut in the bedroom**. It is outside of the bedroom where most women have problems with that sort of treatment."*

Then why don't women simply choose to interact with Alpha male types exclusively? Here are a few reasons why (note: some of these reasons have already been highlighted in previous chapters, so they may appear to be repetitive):

- Most Alpha male types, and particularly *Total Alpha male* types, do not like to spend time with women in any sort of non-physical, non-sexual manner; Many women eventually find this trait to be very frustrating; also, the vast majority of *Total Alpha male* types are very hard to get along with personality wise on a day-to-day basis (mainly because they always expect to have their way)

- Along the lines of the first point above, Alpha male types are not really into spending a lot of time flattering women, entertaining women, and/or listening to women 'whine and complain' about the various problems in their life; Alpha male types feel like they have better things to do with their free time;

- Most Alpha male types either **a)** do not earn as much money as many Beta male types do, or **b)** if they do earn a decent amount of money, they are going to spend it on multiple women as opposed to just one *(e.g., if an Alpha male type has say $10,000 to spend on women, then he is going to spend an average of $500 on 20 women or maybe $1,000 on 10 women rather than spend $10,000 on one woman)*;

- Most Alpha male types, with the possible exception of those who are maybe 40 years of age or older, are never going to commit themselves to remaining faithfully monogamous to just one woman indefinitely. Alpha male types are almost always going to be invited by multiple women to engage in sexual activities frequently giving these men more than their fair share of options for female companionship.

Alpha male types in today's society simply have no motivation to 'woo' and 'court' a woman. For what reason? The sexual appeal of an Alpha male is just in a woman's nature and has been for centuries ... even before the days of fancy, expensive cars, and six-figure incomes.

And because of the Beta Male Revolution, even the vast majority of Beta male types are no longer interested in lengthy courtships with women, unless they know for a fact that those women are very prudish and monogamy-oriented, and have never, ever engaged in sexual relations with multiple Alpha male types.

If you are very observant, you will notice something about many women. When an Alpha male type invites them to engage in a few episodes of short-term and/or non-monogamous 'casual' sex, even if those women are not interested, they will usually respond with a lighthearted reaction of, "you are SO BAD ... you are naughty. You're a bad boy!"

Conversely, when a woman perceives a man to be more of a Beta male type, and that man expresses an interest in only indulging in short-term, non-monogamous type sex, many women will behave as though they are "offended" and "insulted." They will quite frequently have a very 'negative' reaction to a Beta male type's sexual advances. There is a simple reason for that along the lines of everything I have been discussing.

Women don't mind engaging in short-term and/or non-monogamous sex with Alpha male types because they firmly believe that they are going to enjoy themselves just as much if not more than the men are. They confidently assume that the Alpha male types are going to do a thorough job of leaving them feeling pleased and totally satisfied in bed.

Women do not feel the same way about Beta male types sexually. Most women feel like they are going to be bored to death in bed with a Beta male type. They feel like these men are not going to do an adequate job of leaving them feeling pleased and satisfied in bed. Many women have been known to 'fake' their orgasms with Beta male types just so that they can end the sex session as soon as possible. It usually takes a lot longer for a Beta male type to 'get a woman in the mood' than it does for an Alpha male type to do the same. Female sex toys were created for women who experience unsatisfying sex with Beta male types.

Have you noticed that just about all Beta male types tend to express comments like, "Women are simply not as interested in sex as men are!" or "I don't think women really like sex! It's us men who are always horny!!" **Yeah, RIGHT.** You will never hear an Alpha male express such comments. **Never.** Women are always horny to engage in sex with an Alpha male type. **Always.** Women do not make Alpha males 'jump through hoops' as a prerequisite for getting in their pants. That is a tactic specifically reserved for Beta male types.

Secondly, most women tend to assume that Beta male types are going to be much more willing to offer a woman of interest their non-sexual attention and companionship and access to their financial resources in exchange for that woman's sexual attention and companionship. This is what the vast majority of women who are manipulative, materialistic, and sexually duplicitous bank on.

When a man who a woman perceives to be a Beta male type refuses to offer either one (financial assistance and support AND/OR long-term monogamy), women become **VERY ANGRY.** The reality of women is simply this: most women who possess promiscuous and/or polyamorous tendencies don't mind a *Total Alpha male* type treating them like a 'kinky slut' because of the simple fact that they view *Total Alpha male* types in the **exact same way.** Women do not usually want *Total Alpha male* types as their next husband or next long-term boyfriend. They just want those guys for a convenient "kinky roll in the hay" whenever they are horny and in the mood for sex.

So that is why it does not tick women off when a *Total Alpha male* type (or even, in most cases, an *Alpha male with a few Beta traits and tendencies* who happens to married, engaged, or has a long-term girlfriend already) objectifies them and treats them as 'just sex objects.' With Alpha male types, **the feeling is usually mutual** among women.

Before the days of the MANosphere, and before the days of the Beta Male Revolution, many women felt like they could 'sow their wild oats' with Alpha male types between the ages of roughly 18 and 24 or between 18 and 29, and then find a nice, sweet, polite, financially self-sufficient, monogamy-oriented Beta male type once they turned 30.

This is no longer the case.

Another thing about the idea of a man 'courting' and 'wooing' a woman: men – neither Alpha male types or Beta male types – have never really been interested in 'courting' a woman when their objective was just sexual companionship, and sexual companionship only. Any woman who believes otherwise is very naïve and delusional.

Men from my father's generation and grandfather's generation 'wooed' and 'courted' women because the position of 'wife' was similar to a company or corporation recruiting a college graduate to become a prized employee who they confidently assumed would make their company more productive and profitable.

Before the 1960s, a wife was viewed as way more than simply a 'female companion' or an attractive 'sex partner.' Usually, a man's wife was a combination of this for a man:

- A virgin entering into the marriage
- The biological mother of his children
- The children's nurturer, baby-sitter, and nanny
- His personal chef and meal preparer
- His household organizer and maid
- His educational tutor for his children
- His personal accountant for his household finances
- His grocery shopper and clothing shopper
- His errand runner
- His overall personal assistant

So, when a woman agreed to be a man's wife, it was similar to a woman accepting a company's offer of employment. A man's wife was almost similar to her being his 'employee' (who he would frequently engage in sexual activities with) and romantic companion rather than just his romantic companion alone. **A man's wife was expected to bring a lot to the table**.

In return, the man took care of all of the woman's financial needs and obligations and generally treated her like a 'Queen' of sorts to keep her motivated to continue performing those various duties listed above for him and his children.

In today's society, very few women are willing to be a 'stay-at-home mother' and 'housewife' for a man. Many women no longer cook for men, and most women have jobs and careers. Matter of fact, in today's society, the roles of men and women have actually been 'flipped' in some households. Over the years, I have met men who were 'stay-at-home fathers' and 'house husbands.' If that situation works out for the men and women involved more power to them.

The dictionary definition of 'woo' is *"to seek the affection or love of someone ... especially when the objective is marriage."* The definition of 'court' is essentially the same.

What many women need to understand is that marriage is an **honor** and a **privilege**. It is not a legally mandated 'right.' A woman has to prove herself as exceptionally worthy of being called a man's 'wife.' Some women foolishly believe that as long as they are physically attractive and possess a high degree of sex appeal, that this means that they should automatically have many men beating down their door begging to marry them.

Well, if you are a woman reading this ... and you're honest enough to admit that you fall into that category ... **this paperback is your wake-up call**.

So, bottom line, if you are a woman reading this, you need to stop thinking about what men should have to offer you ... and instead, ask yourself, **what do you have to offer men?** Forget about your looks. Forget about your ability to please and satisfy a man sexually. What do you have to offer him beyond those two factors? Think long and hard on that question. Your answers to this question will help you understand why you have never received a marriage proposal from a man in your adult life.

One principle I usually share with my male clients is this:

When it comes to short-term and/or non-monogamous sexual relationships between men and women, men are usually the 'sellers,' and women are usually the 'buyers.' A man becomes a prolific womanizer not because he CHOSE TO BE ... but more so, because he was CHOSEN TO BE by a number of different women who were interested in his sexual prowess.

In contrast, when it comes to long-term strictly monogamous sexual relationships, women then become the 'sellers' and men are the very selective 'buyers.' No woman can really 'choose' to become a man's wife (unless she is dealing with a very wimpy type Beta male type, and she knows that she can simply 'demand' that this man proposes marriage to her).

Generally speaking, **men select women** to become their long-term girlfriend, their fiancée, and their wife.

Men ... always keep this in mind when you hear a woman 'whining and complaining' about the womanizing ways of an Alpha male: Have you ever 'whined and complained' on a day-to-day, week-to-week, month-to-month basis about a woman who you had absolutely, positively no interest in sharing her company in a romantic and/or sexual manner? Honestly?

99.999% chance, no you have not. As human beings, we rarely if ever whine and complain about the behavior of people who we want nothing to do with. Typically, if we have no interest in spending time with someone, and they have an irritating personality or exhibit behavior that we feel we cannot tolerate, we simply leave that person alone and never, ever speak to them again. End of story.

Our natural tendency as men and women is only to whine and complain about undesirable behavior that is being exhibited by a man or woman who we are really interested in spending time with. Particularly, men or women who we want to spend time with in a romantic or sexual manner.

Speaking of desirable vs. undesirable behavior, one scenario Beta males tend to experience quite often is one in which a woman exhibits pleasant behavior before she gets married, but then turns into the "bitch from Hell" after the marriage begins. This is called the 'marital bait-and-switch.'

Continue reading my friend.

Chapter Thirteen

Reality #4 of Today's Dating Scene:

Many Beta Males are Dreadfully Afraid of What is Referred to as the

'Marital Bait-and-Switch' Routine

I interviewed a guest on my talk radio show earlier this year, and one of the things he discussed was his ten-year marriage that ended in divorce. Most men in today's society view divorce proceedings as something that benefits women far more than it benefits men, and this has left a lot of men in society frustrated.

For some Beta male types who earn who earn a six figure or seven figure income, they are leaning toward having a prenuptial agreement in place before exchanging vows. For other men, they simply have very little desire to enter into marriage at all.

This particular guest of mine described what he felt was what I refer to as a 'marital bait-and-switch' by his ex-wife. What exactly is a 'marital bait-and-switch?'

First, I feel compelled to repeat an underrated fact I mentioned in an earlier chapter: women do not need to be married or involved in a long-term 'boyfriend-girlfriend' relationship to engage in sexual activities with a man on a regular or semi-regular basis. **Keep this in mind.**

The only exception would be women whose parents forced them to remain a virgin until they were married (which happened quite often before the 1960s). Women in this situation were just as anxious to get married for sexual purposes as the men were.

In today's more open-minded, free-spirited, and erotically uninhibited society, women can engage in sexual activities with a man anytime they desire. So if this is the case for most women, why would any woman still be motivated to get married?

Just last fall, I had a woman as a guest on my show that expressed the comment, *"Alan, I can name at least ten reasons that women want to be in a relationship (with a man) that have nothing to do with sex."* The reason she expressed that comment was because I offered the strong opinion that a desire to have a regular, dependable female sex companion was included in most men's Top 2, Top 3 reasons for wanting to be married or wanting to be in a long-term romantic relationship with a woman.

There is a saying that is often repeated among women that go along the lines of, "Why would a man be motivated to purchase the cow if he can have access to the milk for free?"

There is a high degree of truth and validity to that adage. For most men, and particularly Alpha male types, they lose their motivation to become a woman's husband, fiancé, or long-term boyfriend if they know they can have sex with that woman regularly in a non-monogamous context.

Next to the desire to engage in regular sex with a woman, most men's primary motivation for entering into marriage or a long-term monogamous relationship with a woman is to prevent other men from flirting with or making sexual advances toward a woman who they enjoy having sex with and really care about.

Let me make this clear: There is nothing 'wrong' per se about sex being a low priority in a long-term relationship or marriage, as long as both the man and the woman involved in the relationship or marriage **know that upfront**.

I always tell my male and female clients: I can tolerate just about any relationship **as long as I know what the expectations are at the very beginning of the relationship**.

I do not like unpleasant 'surprises,' and I believe I speak for a good majority of the men in society. Most men I know have no interest in being a woman's 'platonic husband' or 'platonic boyfriend' unless that is a role that they agreed to adhere to at the outset of the relationship or marriage.

Let's be real: if you take away a woman's ability and willingness to please and satisfy a man sexually and help him experience pleasurable orgasms, many men would never speak to another woman for the remainder of their adult life. For some men, the desire for sex is as high as 95% of the reason why men even bother talking to women or socially interacting with them.

Thinking about the comment expressed by my female guest, I will offer my Top 10 reasons why many women maintain a strong desire to get married that have nothing to do with a desire to engage in sexual activities with a man on a regular basis:

1. So that they can feel better about giving birth to one or more children and avoid having multiple children out of wedlock;

2. To make their parents and relatives happy;

3. To prove to their girlfriends that there is at least one man on Earth that wants their companionship for more than just her ability to please him sexually;

4. To be in a position to have someone to take care of their financial obligations and expenses if they do not have a job or are in-between jobs;

5. To have a male companion to engage in entertaining conversation with on a daily or weekly basis;

6. To experience the excitement of participating in a wedding ceremony and wearing a bridal gown;

7. To have someone to regularly accompany them to various social events, travel destinations, movies, concerts, restaurant meals, etc.;

8. To have someone to assist them with the day-to-day responsibilities of raising one or more children;

9. To have a dependable 'shoulder to cry on' and an 'empathetic listener ear' when they are dejected, depressed, sad, frustrated, angry, etc.

10. To have someone in their life to make them feel beautiful and sexy when their looks begin to fade, and their sex appeal begins to diminish as a result of getting older and/or adding a significant amount of body weight (this is known as 'hitting the wall');

There you have it. Matter of fact, I actually wrote a freelance article for my men's dating advice column in December 2014 where I discussed an 'informal survey' I conducted on an online matchmaking service and do you know that 59 of the 147 women who I surveyed (roughly 40%) said that sex was the "least of their priorities" for wanting to find a long-term boyfriend and/or future husband. Many of those 59 women said that if they only engaged in sexual activities an average of 5-10 times per year, they would be content. I found those responses mind-blowing.

Name one heterosexual man you know who wants to be married to engage in sexual activities an average of five-to-ten times per year? I have never met a man who was under the age of 60 who would be content with an almost non-existent sex life. Hell, with erectile dysfunction pills available, even men 60 years of age and older would not be content with such minimal sex with their spouse.

The main problem I had with these 59 women on that dating site is that none of them made it specifically clear in their online profiles that sex was not important to them. None of these women had a sentence in their profiles where they stated clearly, "I am not looking for a male companion to engage in regular sex with. Sex is not that important to me."

This goes back to the notion of the 'marital bait-and-switch' concept. The male guest I had on my show mentioned that he suffered through a 'sexless marriage' during the last five years of his ten-year marriage. Five years without any sex with his wife?!? Unbelievable. In the last couple of decades, the problem of 'sexless marriages' is becoming more and more prevalent (and in fairness to women, it is not just men; many women have been denied sex by their husbands too).

What was interesting is that this particular male guest admitted that throughout most of his marriage, he exhibited the behavior of a Beta male rather than an Alpha male (what was also interesting is that this guy is 6'4" ... and some men foolishly believe that any man who is six feet tall or taller are all Alpha male types. Wrong!)

He said that before getting married, his ex-wife was extremely affectionate and more-than-willing to engage in sexual activities with him whenever he wanted to. Then, once the two got married, he said her behavior toward him slowly but surely began to change (for the worst).

This scenario is a major fear for men regarding the idea of getting married, and particularly among Beta male types. Next to the fear of having to give up half of their financial and material assets because of divorce, nothing scares men away from marriage more than the thought of their wife exhibiting behavior after their wedding day that is totally different than the behavior that their wife exhibited before their wedding day.

This is one of the reasons why I always tell male clients that they should avoid going out of their way to present themselves to women as 'easy to get along with' in the early stages of dating. I feel like this is a huge mistake.

On one end, I do not think that a man should be purposefully 'antagonistic' with his long-term girlfriend or fiancée, but at the same time, he should never 'hold back' his real feelings and strong opinions from his girlfriend or fiancée either for the specific purpose of preventing a heated disagreement.

As a man, you want always want to force a woman to reveal her 'real side' to you in the early stages of your relationship with a woman. You never want a woman to be able to maintain a disingenuous façade throughout the entire course of your premarital relationship with her, only for her to unleash a side of her personality and behavior during the marriage that you have never, ever witnessed before.

There are some women I have met over the years who have openly admitted to me that they more or less 'played a role' before getting married because they did not want their 'real behavior' to scare their fiancé away. For example, many women confessed to me that they kept their 'argumentative side' or their penchant for behaving like a 'spoiled princess' in check prior to getting married.

I do not believe any man should propose marriage to a woman until he has been in a romantic relationship with that woman for a minimum of eighteen months, and preferably two or three years. Once you know you are entertaining the thought of proposing marriage to a woman, take the time to *really talk to that woman* and find out who she **really** is (and not who she may be 'pretending' to be just to motivate you to marry her).

An alternative title for 'spouse' among many men and women is 'life partner.' If you plan on sharing your place of residence with someone for the remainder of your adult life ... always make sure that there will be no 'unpleasant surprises' at any point in your marriage. That is, assuming, you are bold enough to go ahead and decide even to propose marriage to this woman.

In my next-to-last chapter, I am going to discuss how many men are very reluctant to marry a woman who is older, divorced, or has multiple children out of wedlock. This is a very controversial issue for many women, but it is an issue that is frequently discussed on many blog sites in the MANosphere.

Continue reading my friend.

Chapter Fourteen

Reality #5 of Today's Dating Scene:

Many Men Who Have Never Been Married and Do Not Have Children Can Afford to be 'Nitpicky' When Choosing a Wife

I remember when I was in my twenties, my mother and I were having a conversation about dating, relationships, and marriage. At the time, I had just broken up with my college sweetheart, and she was offering me some 'motherly advice' regarding how she felt I should proceed with dating women from that point forward.

Later in the conversation, she offered the comment, "Men have it easy when it comes to dating as it relates to age. Women cannot wait too long to get married because it lowers their stock value if their husband wants his wife to have multiple children. In my generation, once you reached the age of 30, your stock value would drop for each year you advanced past 30 as far as being a prime candidate to be a man's wife." *She went on to say that once a woman reached the age of 40, her 'stock value' was really going to diminish unless the man she was dating was divorced or widowed, and already had children by another woman (or he was not interested in raising children).*

I remember I was exchanging messages with a fellow dating coach via the internet once, and he asked me, *"Alan, who is your primary demographic?"* I responded, "Single heterosexual men of all ages and backgrounds and to a lesser extent, women who are both single and in a relationship or married. Why do you ask?" He then asked, *"If you don't mind me asking ... are you earning six figures or more as a professional dating coach?"* I responded, "LOL. Not at this time. What made you ask me that?" Finally, he wrote, *"Because you talk about a lot of controversial and raunchy stuff!! LOL. My primary demographic is women 30 years of age or older who are looking to find a husband and get married. They would perceive some of the stuff you discuss on your talk radio program as being too centered on casual sex and one-night stands and stuff. The women in my demographic are not looking for anything short-term or casual. They are looking to find a husband! They want men who are willing to commit!"*

This particular dating coach who wrote me was and still is earning a six-figure salary from his many female clients. A lot of male dating coaches who cater to women are earning large salaries from their eBooks, paperbacks, hardcovers, audiobooks, consultation sessions, CDs, DVDs, and other products and services. Good for them.

If you were to ask most men who are actively a part of the MANosphere why this is, they would very quickly offer an opinion along the lines of, "Because those guys are giving these naïve women 'blue pill' type advice. They are feeding these women's heads with 'romantic fairytales' and unrealistic / idealistic type advice. Once a woman reaches a certain age, her SMV ('sexual marketplace value' or 'social market value') drops drastically. Women need to wake up and realize this."

One reason why a lot of women, particularly hardcore feminist types, pretty much despise and hate the MANosphere and all it stands for, is because of three primary reasons:

1. Most of the men who subscribe to the advice offered by the MANosphere seem to be 'anti-marriage';

2. Most of the men who subscribe to the advice offered by the MANosphere view women as 'sex objects,' and seem only to be interested in short-term and/or non-monogamous 'casual' sex relationships with women;

3. **Many** of the popular bloggers and dating advice gurus in the MANosphere have harsh criticisms of the idea of dating women who are older, obese, divorced, or have given birth to two or more children outside the context of marriage

Point #3 really gets women riled up. Many women who are 45 years of age still want to believe that they have the same appeal to men that they did when they were 25 or 35, and the reality is, 99% of the time, that is simply not the case.

Since I turned 40, I have dated one woman who was also past the age of 40 in a 'serious' manner. I was 46, and she was 43 at the time. She had one daughter from a previous marriage.

There have been some other women who I have dated in a more 'casual,' non-monogamous manner who were between 40 and 50 since my 40th birthday. All that to say, I do not personally have any sort of major 'aversion' to dating older women, particularly casually and non-monogamously. I find many women who are 40+ to be mature and very sexy.

I have also dated my fair share of younger women as well. When I was 42, I briefly dated a woman who was 23, and I have interacted with a good number of women over the last ten years or so romantically or sexually who were between 30 and 39.

My own dating preferences and past experiences aside, I know many men who absolutely, positively will not consider dating a woman who is 40 years of age or older other than for some variation of short-term and/or non-monogamous 'casual' sex. When it comes to evaluating a woman's potential to be their wife, many older women get immediately crossed off the list.

The exception would be men who are older themselves, divorced or widowed, and either already have one or more children or have no interest in raising children. Many men in this category have no problem dating a middle-aged or older woman in a serious, long-term, monogamous manner.

But for men who have never been married, and currently do not have any children (but they very badly want to raise children), these types are **harsh** toward women who are older, fat / obese, divorced, or have given birth to multiple children out of wedlock. Sometimes, I read some of the comments, and I'm like, "Ouch!! These guys are merciless!!" Yes ladies, it gets THAT bad on some message boards, discussion forums, and blog sites.

In these men's partial defense, some women who are 36 years of age or older tend to express a lot of 'highly selective' and even unrealistic and delusional criteria for the type of man they want as their next boyfriend or future husband. Sometimes, I will listen to women and just shake my head. Like, "This woman has got to be kidding me ..."

Men place as much emphasis on a woman's age, weight, and fertility as many women place on a man's earning potential and income, height, and sexual prowess.

My feeling is this: if a man has never, ever been married, and he has never, ever fathered any children, then that man has a right to be 'nitpicky' regarding his selection of a wife or long-term romantic companion.

I am going to discuss three types of women: Women who are older, women who divorced, and women who already have children (particularly out of wedlock as opposed to children they gave birth to while they were previously married).

WOMEN WHO ARE 36 YEARS OF AGE OR OLDER

According to many studies and surveys, the women who are the most appealing to men for marriage age-wise are women who are between 18 and 29, and in a few cases, 18-35. To use my mother's term of 'stock value' (or again, what many in the MANosphere refer to as a woman's 'sexual marketplace value' or 'social market value'), the first year I would arguably say that a woman's stock value begins to drop significantly would be once she reaches her 36th birthday.

These days, many women are choosing to focus on their college education and their careers in their twenties and most of their thirties, and waiting until later to open themselves up to the idea of getting married. For the sake of placing themselves in a position of becoming financially self-sufficient, I don't blame most of these women. With the exception of professional athletes and Entertainment Industry celebrities, not too many men between the ages of 18 and 35 are in a position to take care of a woman financially and allow her to be a 'stay-at-home mother' and 'housewife.'

For a man who wants to get married, and have his wife give birth to say, three or more children, a woman who is between 36 and 39 is 'risky.' A woman who is 40 years of age or older is almost out of the question.

I have had some women I know who are 36 years of age or older 'brag' to me that they could still grab the attention of a man who is between 18 and 29. I always chuckle. Sometimes, if I want to get them riled up, I will ask, "So … how many marriage proposals have you received from those 'younger men'?" Then they will glare at me or frown, and shut up quickly.

Have you noticed that when you examine many of the women's profiles on some these online matchmaking sites, many will feature a comment such as, "I've had my fun in my twenties and thirties, but I am now tired of games. I am looking for a man who has serious intentions" (or some similar comment). What that means is, "I gravitated toward nothing but Alpha male types between the age of 18 and 35, but now that I am 36 years of age or older, I now want a nice, polite Beta male type who I can train and easily have my way with without engaging in too much sex with."

When it comes to engaging in short-term and/or non-monogamous 'casual' sex ... no man (young or old) is really against the idea of having sex with women who are between 36 and 49. Some young men will even have sex with a 'Sugar Mama' type who is between the ages of 50 and 59.

On the other hand, when it comes to proposing marriage, very few men who are between the ages of 18 and 29 or between the ages of 18 and 35 are going to propose marriage to a woman who is 40 years of age or older.

29 is the latest age women should get married by if they plan on raising a large family (a minimum of three children with their husband). Sometime between 30 and 35 at the absolute latest.

WOMEN WHO ARE DIVORCED

I know many men who will not seriously date a woman who is divorced if they have never been married themselves. Even I had that attitude when I was in my twenties. I had no desire to be in a long-term romantic relationship with a woman who was divorced. Once I got into my thirties, my attitude softened up.

When some men hear the term 'divorced,' they immediately think to themselves, 'this is a woman who *failed* at being married.' Many men perceive a woman who is divorced as being a woman who will bring a lot of 'emotional baggage' into a new relationship with a man, and for most men, 'emotional baggage' is a huge turn-off.

Interesting enough, there are some men who actually favor women who are divorced after a long marriage. In their minds, this means that the woman was not just out in society 'sowing her wild oats' with a high number of womanizing Alpha male types. So, they would prefer to get into a relationship with a woman who got married at say, the age of 23 and was divorced by the age of 32 or 33. Especially if that woman did not give birth to any children while she was married the first time.

Many MANosphere advisors and gurus will often remark, "When you date a woman who is divorced, you are allowing her to bring all of her bad habits and preconceived notions of how marriage 'should be' into a new relationship with you."

That attitude is not 100% valid, but it is also not totally invalid either. It just really depends on how mature the woman is, and if she is the type that can learn from her past mistakes.

I say if a man who has never been married decides that being in a long-term relationship with a divorced woman is not for him, that is totally his choice. He has the right to be 'selective' if he so chooses. No woman can validly criticize him for being a bit too 'nitpicky' in his selection of a potential wife.

WOMEN WITH MULTIPLE CHILDREN OUT OF WEDLOCK

I would say that next to women who men consider to be 'morbidly obese' (women who are approximately 50-75 pounds or more above her 'ideal weight'), there is no bigger turn-off to men in the MANosphere than women who have given birth to two or more children outside the context of marriage.

Why?

Because most men (and especially Beta male types) view this as a clear-cut sign that a woman has been 'sowing her wild oats' with *Total Alpha male* types (or *Alpha males with a few Beta traits and tendencies* types when she was younger).

This was included in many early definitions of a 'Beta male' in the early years of the MANosphere. Most men would describe a Beta male as a "man who is willing to help a woman raise children that are the offspring of one or more Alpha males" (That is also the formal definition of a 'Cuckold'; A true Cuckold is a man who is married, but after his wife commits adultery and gets pregnant by an Alpha male, that man is willing to remain with his wife and raise that Alpha male's son or daughter as if it were his own son or daughter).

This perception of how Beta males are, or at least used to be, leaves many Beta male types angry and bitter in today's society. Consequently, many Beta male types today will avoid dating women with children out of wedlock as if those women have a contagious disease.

As mentioned in Part One of this paperback, before 1960, it was considered extremely 'shameful' for a woman to give birth to a child out of wedlock. Some parents would disown their daughter if she got pregnant without being married.

Even in today's society, in some upper middle-class families, many mothers and fathers will strictly forbid their daughters from getting pregnant outside the context of marriage. They feel it would bring some degree of embarrassment to their family.

I say this: if you feel like you thoroughly enjoy a woman's company, and you get along very well with a woman's son(s) and/or daughter(s) ... then don't worry about what 'other people' will think of you dating this woman. If it makes you happy, go for it. If a woman having children out of wedlock is not causing any problems for you, that is all that matters.

In regard to the women reading this, just be conscious of the fact that if you have already given birth to two or more children out of wedlock, a lot of men who have never been married and do not have any children of their own are going to be unenthusiastic about entering into any long-term, emotionally profound, monogamous relationship with you.

In fairness to women, I also know a lot of single women who have never been married and do not have any children who have no desire to marry a man who has two or more children by women who he was not married to at the time those women gave birth to his children.

The reality is, all of us ... young men, older men, young women, older women ... have our unique list of 'selective criteria' that will cause us to cross someone off our list of potential marriage partners. If I had to publicly name two of my 'deal-breakers', it would be cigarette smoking and habitual drug use (not including marijuana). I cannot stand the smell of cigarette smoke, and I have no desire to date a woman who has some sort of cocaine habit or heroin addiction. I always let women know this in my first or second conversation with them.

In my very next chapter – my last – I am going to discuss how Beta male types have grown to become so distrustful and wary of women's duplicitous and fickle ways, that they just don't view many women as 'marriage material' any longer.

Many men who used to be the biggest defenders of women's character and integrity are now some of the harshest critics of women and some of the nation's most bitter misogynists. I will touch on this and a few other things in my very last chapter.

Continue reading my friend.

Chapter Fifteen

Reality #6 of Today's Dating Scene:
Many Beta Male Types Who Previously Adored, Defended, and Worshipped Women Now HATE Them

Which men have seen their behavior change the most since 1960? Which men's attitudes toward women have changed the least since 1960? Well, let me offer my strong opinions.

TOTAL ALPHA MALES

Before the eras of modern agriculture and modern technology came into play in society, men who were *Total Alpha male* types were the men who were the bravest and most highly masculine. These were the men that women gravitated toward to prevent themselves from being harmed or raped (you have to remember … rape was not always illegal).

Men in this category were always promiscuous and/or polyamorous to some degree, and even if they were married, their wives usually permitted them to take on an additional lover or two as long as the husbands promised not to get those women pregnant or replace their wives with one of their mistresses.

Women rarely have attempted to disrespect these type of men or exhibit spoiled or argumentative behavior with these men. They knew these men were the most confident, the most fearless, the most masculine, and the most likely to erotically dominate them and leave them totally satisfied sexually.

Now that rape is illegal, and women do not necessarily need a man to physically protect them, the men in this category are not as highly sought after to be women's husbands, but they are still highly sought after to be a woman's casual lover or 'lover-on-the-side' in the event that the woman is married or otherwise romantically involved.

The attitude toward women among men in this category is the same as it was in 1960, 1970, or 1980 and beyond. These men know they are in demand sexually (particularly when they are between 15 and roughly 49), and they will always be in demand by a large number of women.

Therefore, men in this category do not have any 'negative' feelings toward women. Why would they? Most men in this category pretty much have their way with women sexually, and never really seek to enter into strictly monogamous marriages or strictly monogamous long-term romantic relationships with women. *Total Alpha male* types in today's society are usually only interested in promiscuous and/or polyamorous sex with women.

I would argue that men in this category have changed **the least** regarding their general attitudes toward women. Most women will never admit this publicly, but **women want men in this category to remain promiscuous and polyamorous**. Women would be heartbroken if *Total Alpha male* types ever developed a 'strictly monogamous' mindset.

ALPHA MALES with a few BETA traits and tendencies

I would make the argument that it was the men in this category that most fueled a lot of the anger and frustration experienced by women between 1900 and 1959.

It was the men in this category that were guiltiest of committing adultery behind their wife's back or divorcing their older wives and replacing them with much younger wives.

Generally speaking, men in this category have always been the most deceitful and duplicitous (meaning, they were privately womanizers, but publicly they sought to give their wives the misleading impression that they were dedicated to being a 'one-woman man'), and duplicity always leaves men and women feeling frustrated and bitter in the long run.

235

Once the Second Wave of Feminism in the 1960s and 1970s helped a lot of 'frustrated wives' and 'frustrated mistresses' accomplish a lot of their goals and objectives in society, these men were forced to become a bit savvier if they still wanted to 'have their cake and eat it too.' Many married men in this category still have mistresses, but they are much more private and discreet about it. The internet and social media make it a lot more challenging for men to remain so duplicitous.

When it comes to indulging in non-monogamous 'casual' sex with women, men in this category do not have any harsh criticisms of women today. When it comes to marriage, men in this category realize that women usually have the 'edge' when it comes to divorce and child custody, but because these men want to have a family and raise children, they just grin and bear it. Sometimes, men in this category are married to women who earn more money than them, so they are not really afraid of being 'taken to the cleaners' if they get divorced.

Bottom line, the behavior of the men in this category has not changed TOO much, but their attitude toward women could be categorized as a wee bit more 'critical' of women who are known to be hardcore feminist types. Men in this category feel like feminist types and blatant misandrists are basically attempting to 'force' them to become more 'Beta' like than

'Alpha' when it comes to marriage, and they do not like it one bit.

BETA MALES with a few ALPHA traits and tendencies

Men in this category did not stand out too much before the agricultural era and the modern technology era. Now, because of Wall Street on the East Coast and the Silicon Valley on the West Coast, there are a lot of 'shy, introverted' types as well as 'mama's boy' types who are now earning six and seven figure incomes and living in huge houses.

The 'good news' is, because of their wealth, men in this category have become much more appealing to women and sought after by women. The 'bad news' is, in most cases, it is ONLY their wealth that many of these women want. Sexually, a lot of women who date and marry men in this category are cheating on them with a *Total Alpha male* type or an *Alpha male with a few Beta traits and tendencies* type behind their back unbeknownst to them.

Before the days of the MANosphere, most of the men in this category had no clue about the manipulative ways of women and the sexually duplicitous ways of women. They believed that the women who dated them and married them were genuinely attracted to them because of their charm, their personality, and their monogamy-oriented and family-oriented intentions. Think about 'Kevin' from the Preface chapter.

Now, because of the MANosphere, men in this category have become very distrustful of women. Many men in this category now view women as 'closet gold diggers' and 'calculating and discreet adulterers.'

Many men in this category are now choosing to 'fight fire with fire.' They will get married to a woman just for the sake of having children, but they will cheat on their wife with one or two mistresses behind their back. The problem is, whenever they get caught cheating, women are taking them to the cleaners during divorce court proceedings and child custody proceedings.

Some of the men in this category are avoiding marriage altogether, and opting for one of the 'alternative relationships' I mentioned in Chapter Ten. Most notably, the 'Sugar Daddy-Sugar Baby' type arrangement.

Before 1960, men in this category were considered the "good men." The men who women could depend on to be financially responsible, remain faithfully monogamous, and do everything possible to please a woman, accommodate a woman, and generally treat her like a 'Queen.'

In today's society, if a man in this category cannot find him a virgin or some religious woman who is between the ages of 18 and 24 who would never give in to her promiscuous and/or polyamorous temptations, the men in this category have pretty much have given up on the idea of marriage. Prenuptial agreements are their best friend.

TOTAL BETA MALES

Hands down, there is no group of men who have angrier, bitter, and more blatantly misogynistic feelings toward women in today's society than the men in this category. The ironic thing is, men in this group usually start out as women's greatest defenders and allies.

Men in this category, when they are in high school or college, usually worship the ground women walk on. These men would be willing to do ANYTHING to please a woman and gain the opportunity to share a woman's company. Even in a purely platonic manner (initially).

If there are at least two romantic dramas you have to view if you want to understand the plight of the *Total Beta male* type, it would have to be **The Last American Virgin** *(1982)* and **Two Lovers** *(2008)*. Actors Lawrence Monoson ("Gary" in *The Last American Virgin*) and Joaquin Phoenix ("Leonard" in *Two Lovers*) both portray two 'White Knight' / 'Captain Save-a-Ho' types in those two films. Sure enough, both films end with those two characters having their heart broken by two women who they have fallen in love with. Phoenix is also good in a similar role in the film **Her** *(2013)*.

This is what happens with *Total Beta male* types. It usually starts when they develop a 'crush' on a girl who doesn't know they exist. Then, if they are lucky, the girl who they have a crush on warms up to them in a purely platonic manner and begins treating them like a 'play brother' or 'male girlfriend.'

The girl / woman will begin complaining about how much she 'hates' Alpha male types (or what she will usually refer to as 'jerks,' 'bad boys,' or 'no good men'), and that she is really looking for a 'nice, sweet guy' who will treat her with 'respect' and 'kindness.' She will say, "Why can't I find a good man?!?"

So, this naive *Total Beta male* type will fall for this manipulative routine hook, line, and sinker. Men in this category truly believe that these girls / women are truly looking for the 'nice guy' to rescue them from those disrespectful 'bad boys.'

Riiiiiiiiiiiiiiiiiiiiiiiiiiiiight. Poor guys. Bless their hearts.

It is usually not until these men have had their heart broken by at least two or three women, or until they became a subscriber to the MANosphere, that they are forced to wake the f**k up.

The reality is, women never want the 'nice guy' for sexual enjoyment and satisfaction purposes. **Never**. To flatter them? **Sure**. To entertain them? **Sure**. To spend money on them? **Sure**. To help them fix their car or vacuum cleaner? **Sure**. To listen to them 'whine and complain' about how an Alpha male type ejaculated semen into their mouth during oral sex without asking their permission first? **Sure**. Get the picture?

The problem with some of the men in this category is that not only have many men in this category changed their attitude toward women, but it has changed very much **for the worst**.

Many men in this category literally and passionately **hate women** now. Some of the men in this category who are mentally and emotionally unstable want to see women harmed, tortured, raped, and even murdered. Yes, these men hate women **that much**. These men are thinking, "You are NOTHING like my sweet, loving mother or grandmother!! She would never, ever treat a man like this!!" Well, of course your mother or grandmother is not going to share the story of the time the Alpha male ejaculated semen in her mouth and then said, "What is your name again?"

In their minds, *Total Beta male* types cannot process or comprehend how a woman could be attracted to an Alpha male type (that dastardly "wolf in sheep's clothing") who treats women 'badly' and cheats on women regularly. They simply do not understand this way of thinking on behalf of women.

For these men, it would be like observing a child who is being mentally, emotionally, and physically abused by his or her biological parents being offered to move in with a new set of foster parents or step-parents who are committed to treating the child with the utmost of care, love, and respect ... and that child declines the offer and elects to remain with the biological parents that are hell bent on continuing to abuse and mistreat them.

Are you familiar with what is known as 'Stockholm Syndrome?' If not, this is when a person is kidnapped and held hostage ... and after a period of weeks, months, or years, the man or woman who is being held captive begins to develop an emotional connection with their kidnappers to the extent that they no longer want to be released.

This is how many *Total Beta male* types view women who gravitate toward Alpha male types. They perceive Alpha male types as the 'abusers' of a woman's emotions, which in their mind, makes Alpha male types the 'worst of the worst.'

The reality is, Alpha male types are not usually 'bad' or mean-spirited toward women at all. An Alpha male's main 'weakness,' if you want to even call it that, is simply that his sexual companionship is desired by more than his fair share of women. I mean, he can't help it if he always has 5-10 women who want to offer him their sexual companionship without requiring that he spend any significant amount of money on these women or without requiring that he promise them any long-term monogamy.

A *Total Alpha male* type and the *Alpha males with a few Beta traits and tendencies* type are just taking advantage of what is being offered to them. Now between the two, the *Alpha males with a few Beta traits and tendencies* are the more deceitful and duplicitous of the two Alpha male types, but even when they cheat or commit adultery, their female companions rarely divorce them or break up with them (because, among other things, the sex is usually too good to give up).

Some of my male clients are currently in the *Total Beta male* category, and I am doing everything possible to help them upgrade to the status of a *Total Alpha male*, an *Alpha male with a few Beta traits and tendencies*, or at bare minimum, a *Beta male with a few Alpha traits and tendencies*. It is a challenge, but one I am up for.

Trust me … no (heterosexual) man wants to remain indefinitely in the category of a *Total Beta male*.

What women will be most negatively affected by this 'Beta Male Revolution' that is currently going on?

Some women will not be affected by The BETA MALE REVOLUTION at all, just like not too many *Total Alpha male* types were negatively affected by the Second Wave of Feminism and the Sexual Revolution in the 1960s and 1970s. Surely, a certain percentage of women will be negatively affected by men's growing change in attitude and behavior. Among those . . .

- Women who are 36 years of age or older, who have never been married and have no children, who are very much looking to get married and have children with a man earning a six or seven figure salary;

- Women who are 36 years of age or older, who already have children, who very much want to get married to a man earning a six or seven figure salary;

- Women who are not virgins, but are expecting men to wait weeks, months, or years before engaging in sexual activities for the first time ... and even worse, women who are not virgins who expect men to wait until marriage to engage in sex for the first time;

- Women who are divorced and have children, and have their sights set on marrying a man who has never been married and has no children ... and especially if the man is younger than the woman;

- Women who have gotten away with cheating on their boyfriend or husband behind their back regularly

- Last, but not least, women who have a history of accumulating a high number of 'purely platonic male friends' who were more than willing to function as these women's 'play brother' or 'male girlfriend' for an indefinite period without complaint.

If 1960-1979 were the defining decades for Feminism and the Sexual Revolution, then I would argue that 2005-2024 (and maybe beyond) will be the defining period for The Beta Male Revolution.

First, it was women who angrily reacted to men's chauvinistic, sexist, disloyal, and sexually duplicitous ways ... and now it is men angrily reacting to women's female chauvinism, feminist-oriented sexism, their blatant materialism in marriage, and their highly manipulative and sexually duplicitous ways.

Now, men feel like it is **their turn**. Men want more rights as it relates to abortion, alimony, divorce, child custody, child support, and reclaiming their sense of manhood and masculinity. And secondly, men are making every effort to call out and expose women who they view as 'closet gold digger' types and lying, cheating girlfriend and adulterous wife types.

For many reasons already mentioned earlier in this chapter, the reason I did not title this paperback simply, "The Male Revolution" is because the vast majority of Alpha male types could care less about the rantings of feminists and other romantically and sexually frustrated women in society.

If a woman is bisexual or heterosexual, constantly horny for sex, and loves to indulge in many episodes of hot, kinky, non-monogamous sex while being erotically dominated by a male sex partner, then Alpha male types will always be in demand. And these men know it. They are content with their status in today's dating scene.

The only way an Alpha male type would ever become frustrated is if you placed him in a social environment where it was mandatory that all of the men and women in that particular social environment had to remain indefinitely monogamous to their spouses or romantic companions. Otherwise, Alpha males will always receive more than their fair share of sexual attention from women.

Alpha male types always knew the 'games' women play with men. Most Alpha male types, such as street pimps, always knew that women were never as 'innocent,' 'prudish,' loyal, and 'monogamy-oriented' as they pretended to be.

Beta male types, on the other hand, did not begin becoming enlightened about the true nature of most women until somewhere between roughly 2001 and 2010. Some, even later than that. I would venture to say for a very small percentage of men, this very paperback will be their first real "wake-up call."

Finally, here is how I choose to sum up all of my thoughts in this paperback:

Summary Point #1: Contrary to what many factions of organized religion will attempt to brainwash you into believing, marriage is a man-made social construct. There is nothing in our biological DNA that creates a natural inclination toward marriage or monogamy.

The idea of monogamy began to be emphasized because of men's insecurity over paternity issues. Many in society felt that monogamous marriages were the closest thing to a DNA paternity test before a DNA paternity test ever existed.

If you religious types want to bring God into the discussion, why would God create marriage, knowing that roughly 50% of the marriages would end in divorce?? That is a blatant insult to the intelligence and wisdom of a Divine Power such as God.

Think about it. If there were 100,000,000 dating singles in the United States, and 55,000,000 of those were single heterosexual women, and 45,000,000 of those were single heterosexual men, how could everyone be monogamous?

That does not even make logical sense. If every single man and single woman aspired to enter into a strictly monogamous marriage, that would mean that 10,000,000 single women would never, ever find a husband. Is that even fair? You tell me.

Summary Point #2: Any relationship can work for a man and a woman involved if they know what the expectations are at the beginning of the relationship. You have to be a bit 'selfish' when deciding what type of relationship works best for you. Long-term? Short-term? Strictly Monogamous? Polyamorous? Wide open and promiscuous? Full of emotional involvement? No emotions involved whatsoever? Only YOU know what type of relationship will work best for you and your particular needs.

Summary Point #3: Before 1960, strictly monogamous marriages worked for many men and women because for all practical purposes, that was the only relationship men and women were able to own up to publicly and socially. That is not the case any longer. Men and women today are much more open-minded, free-spirited, and erotically uninhibited. All men and women need to **own** their sexuality and not concern themselves with who is going to criticize them and pass judgment on them and their behavior behind-their-back.

Summary Point #4: The Beta Male Revolution has shifted into high gear. What does this mean for women? You can no longer execute the routine of sexually interacting with Alpha males, and then later transitioning over to the Beta male types and attempting to convince them that all Alpha male types are the 'mean, abusive, bad guys.' Beta male types know now that this is complete B.S.

If you are a woman who assumes that you can 'sow your wild oats' with a wide assortment of womanizing Alpha males between the ages of 15 and 29, and then think you're simply going to easily end up connecting with a naive, polite, accommodating, and financially generous Beta male 'nice guy' type once you turn 30, you are going to be in for a rude awakening. Beta male types are no longer as naive as they may look thanks to the knowledge, wisdom, and advice offered by the MANosphere.

Beta male types now fully realize just how dishonest and disingenuous many women can be, how misleading and manipulative they can be, and how materialistic and sexually duplicitous they can be. In other words, if you are a woman who loves to engage in manipulative 'head games' with men, most Beta males in today's society **ARE ON TO YOUR GAMES**. They have the 'Beta male manipulation playbook' now. They know what's up. Beta males are gaining more and more knowledge and wisdom about women's true nature each and every week.

Summary Point #5: Similar to Point #4, women who have had a history of accumulating dozens and dozens of flattering and entertaining 'play brothers' and emotionally empathetic and supportive 'male girlfriends' are also going to find themselves becoming very egotistically frustrated in the years to come. Beta male types are no longer willing to 'settle' for being a woman's purely platonic male companion. Not at all. All men want to experience pleasurable orgasms with a woman. Believe that. Men have no desire to *FunClub* with women any longer.

Summary Point #6: Love is not directly synonymous with the idea of monogamy, and similarly, monogamy is not directly synonymous with the idea of getting married. There are men and women involved in openly polyamorous relationships who are very much 'in love.' There are many men and women who are married, but it is more so representative of a purely platonic 'co-parenting arrangement' rather than a marriage that is romantic and sexual in nature. Just like a mother or father is capable of showing love to more than one child, many men and women are also capable of developing a long-lasting emotional connection with more than just one romantic companion or sex partner at a time. You have to do what works best for you.

Summary Point #7: Last but not least, many men and women do not want to be forced to choose one type of companion over another type of companion. Remain realistic about this. Most men want a prudish and monogamy-oriented 'good girl' in their life ... but they also want a couple of kinky and promiscuous and/or polyamorous type women involved in their life too. Either these men are going to be open about this, or they are going to be deceitful about it. Be prepared for the latter.

Similarly, many women want a highly self-assured, very masculine, extremely kinky and erotically dominant lover in their life ... but they are also interested in having another totally different type of man who will be willing to spend time with them for the purpose of flattering them and entertaining them, as well as even a third man who is going to offer them financial assistance and support. Either these women are going to be open and honest about their desire for different types of companions who will serve different purposes for them, or they are going to be deceitful and secretive about it. Realistically, be prepared for the latter.

I hope all of this helps you find the type of meaningful relationship with a member of the opposite sex that you truly desire.

I will offer my closing remarks in the next section, which I refer to as my "Author's Wrap Up & Final Thoughts."

WRAP UP & FINAL THOUGHTS

Promiscuity is not for everyone, Polyamory is not for everyone, and Strict Monogamy is not for everyone. Period.

There is a belief I used to express frequently when I used to post on a website entitled **AskMen.com** years ago. The comment was, "One man's wife, fiancée, or long-term girlfriend is often another man's mistress or casual sex lover."

Most of the men on the AskMen.com discussion forum took heed to the wisdom in that comment and began quoting that comment of mine repeatedly to their friends and acquaintances. Many women would criticize me for expressing such a comment. They would argue that "Good girls are good girls ... and sluts are sluts. There is no mixing of the two." Yeah, right. **That falsehood is what all sexually duplicitous women want most men (and particularly Beta males) to believe**.

One of the reasons why I wrote and self-published my very first book, *Mode One: Let the Women Know What You're REALLY Thinking* was because I realized when I was in my early twenties that most of the women who I found myself socially interacting tended to be *Wholesome Pretender* & *Erotic Hypocrite* types who were very sexually duplicitous.

They would play the role of the 'prudish, monogamy-oriented good girl' when they were in the company of men who they wanted to date long-term and/or marry, but they would reveal their kinkier, promiscuous and/or polyamorous side when they were interacting with kinky, erotically dominant men who they just wanted to exchange pleasurable orgasms with casually.

Consider this paperback as a 'prequel' to either *Mode One* or *The Possibility of Sex*. If there has been one minor 'blessing in disguise' throughout this developing animosity between men and women in society is that it has in many instances created more unity among men of different ethnicities and cultures. Because many men now view manipulative, materialistic, and sexually duplicitous women as the 'common enemy,' many men have put their petty racial differences aside to share knowledge, wisdom, and dating advice with each other. You will always have some degree of blatant racism in many countries and cultures, but at least things are improving.

I believe this paperback is going to be most helpful to many of the 'naïve' Beta male types. Using the Monogamy Island scenario from the Preface, I wrote this book for the clueless 'Kevin' types of the world. For most of the Alpha male types (the 'Tyrone' types of the world), I am preaching to the choir. It has always been my mission to help all single heterosexual men improve their love lives, sex lives, and overall social lives.

Here is what every man and every woman who has taken the time to read this book needs to understand:

For women ... just because a man thoroughly enjoys your sexual attention and companionship does not necessarily mean that this same man has any genuine desire whatsoever for your non-sexual attention and companionship. Keep this in mind. All men who engage in manipulative 'head games' with women do one thing: These men give women the very disingenuous and misleading impression that they have an 'equal interest' in both a woman's sexual and non-sexual companionship when they really just want to spend time with that woman sexually.

For men ... just because a woman thoroughly enjoys your non-sexual attention and companionship and your financial generosity does not necessarily mean that this same woman has any genuine desire whatsoever to engage in sexual activities with you. Keep this in mind. All women who engage in manipulative 'head games' with men are good at doing this: These women love to give men the misleading impression that they have an 'equal interest' in both a man's sexual and non-sexual companionship, when they really just want to be flattered and entertained, and take advantage of whatever financial resources and material possessions that man has to offer them.

As I mentioned in the book, this is related to my personal definition of 'true love.' True love is when you have found someone who satisfies you 100% both sexually and non-sexually. There is no other person you would rather spend time with sexually more than your spouse or romantic companion, and there is no other person in the world that you would rather spend time with non-sexually than your spouse or a romantic companion.

Regarding my female readers, I am always attempting to help them stay away from men who are dangerous and misogynistic, and more specifically men who may be looking to harm them, abuse them, kidnap them, rape them, or date-rape them. I think sexual violence of any kind by a member of any gender is despicable, and I have never been one to condone men behaving in an extremely aggressive manner with women when attempting to have sex with them without those women's expressed consent. I also do not like to see men blatantly leading women on and toying with their emotions unnecessarily.

Plain and simple, I believe 'honesty is the best policy' when it comes to dating and relationships. Men need to quit being deceitful, duplicitous, misleading and manipulative with women, and women need to stop being deceitful, duplicitous, misleading and manipulative with men. The reality of today's society is, discouraging such behavior among dating singles is always easier said than done. I am not at all naïve to this fact.

There was a time when people in society treated a man like he was 'weird' or a homosexual if he was not married and raising a family by the time he was 35. Not in today's society. Again, I am 53 years old, and I do not see myself getting married anytime in the very near future. Long-term monogamy is just not my thing. I am not even sure if an openly polyamorous marriage would be my cup of tea either, but we'll see. Right now, being an 'eternal bachelor' suits me just fine.

For men and women interested in receiving coaching and advice from me, I offer Email consultations, Skype and/or telephone consultations, and one-on-one / face-to-face coaching sessions with men, women, and married & unmarried couples. If you have any questions, contact me at **'coaching@modeone.net'**

Thank you for reading this paperback in its entirety. I really appreciate it, and I sincerely hope it helps you thoroughly understand the motivations and general psychology of various members of the opposite sex. Good luck with your love life, sex life, and social life.

Moooooooooode Ooooooooooone.

Go out and boldly create life-changing opportunities for yourself.

Other Books & Resources I Recommend

http://www.askmen.com

http://www.avoiceformen.com

http://www.TakeBackTheNight.org

http://www.wikipedia.org

http://www.XOXY.com

Black Players: The Secret World of Black Pimps
Dr. Richard Milner & Christina Milner

How to Start a Kinky Relationship: The definitive guide to starting and sustaining a healthy, loving, satisfying alternative relationship – James Amoureux

Men On Strike: Why Men are Boycotting Marriage, Fatherhood, and the American Dream ... and WHY IT MATTERS – Dr. Helen Smith

Marriage, a History: How Love Conquers Marriage
Stephanie Coontz

Alan Roger Currie

PIMP: The Story of My Life
Robert Beck a.k.a. 'Iceberg Slim'

Radical Honesty: How to Transform Your Life by Telling the Truth – Dr. Brad Blanton

Sex at Dawn: How We Mate, Why We Stray, and What It Means for Modern Relationships
Dr. Christopher Ryan and Cacilda Jetha

The Ethical Slut: A Practical Guide to Polyamory, Open Relationships & Other Adventures
Dossie Easton and Janet W. Hardy

The Manipulated Man – Esther Vilar

The Myth of Male Power – Dr. Warren Farrell

The Rational Male – Rollo Tomassi (pseudonym)

The Sugar Daddy Formula: A Sugar Baby's Ultimate Guide to Finding a Wealthy Sugar Daddy
Taylor B. Jones

What Do Women Want? – Daniel Bergner

ABOUT THE AUTHOR

Alan Roger Currie was born and raised in Gary, Indiana and graduated from Indiana University in Bloomington, IN. Currie is the Host of two talk radio podcast programs, *Upfront & Straightforward with Alan Roger Currie* and *The Erotic Conversationalist*. Currie has been interviewed many times on local, regional, and national talk radio programs as well as local, regional and national television talk shows.

Currie, who is known by his female fans, clients, and supporters as "The King of Verbal Seduction" and by his male fans, clients, and supporters as "The Godfather of Verbally Direct Game" has been a featured speaker for various dating & relationships conferences and seduction workshops in various cities in the USA and also in Berlin (Germany) and London (England). Currie works as a professional dating coach for men, and he advises women and married & unmarried couples who are interested in experimenting with the BDSM and/or Polyamory lifestyle.

Currie's main website is **http://www.directapproachdating.com** (for men) and **http://www.modeone.net/training/** (for women and couples)

More biographical information about Alan Roger Currie can be found on **Wikipedia.org**